WRONG PLACE, RIGHT TIME

FOR GERALDINE AND OUR SONS BRIAN AND TONY

WRONG PLACE, RIGHT TIME
Policing the End of Empire

Michael J. Macoun
CMG, OBE, QPM

The Radcliffe Press
London · New York

HV
7911
.M373
A3
1996

Published in 1996 by
The Radcliffe Press
An imprint of I.B.Tauris & Co Ltd
Victoria House
Bloomsbury Square
London WC1B 4DZ

In the United States of America
and Canada distributed by
St Martin's Press
175 Fifth Avenue
New York
NY 10010

A full CIP record for this book is available from the British Library

Library of Congress Catalog card number: available

A full CIP record is available from the Library of Congress

ISBN 1–86064–019–2

Copy-edited and laser-set by Selro Publishing Services, Oxford
Printed and bound in Great Britain by WBC Ltd, Bridgend, Mid Glamorgan

Contents

Contents

Illustrations

Acronyms and Abbreviations

AAA	Amateur Athletic Association
ABA	Amateur Boxing Association
BGR	British Government Representative
BI	British India
BIS	British Information Service
CIA	Central Intelligence Agency
CID	Criminal Investigation Department
CRO	Commonwealth Relations Office
DHV	*Deutscher Handlungsgehilfenverband* (German Commercial Assistants' Union)
DIB	director of the intelligence bureau
DIG	Deputy Inspector-General
DNHV	*Deutscher Nationale Handlungsgehilfenverband*
DOAL	German East Africa Line
DS	Directing Staff
DWS	diplomatic wireless service
FANY	First Aid Nursing Yeomanry
FBI	Federal Bureau of Investigation
FCO	Foreign and Commonwealth Office
GDF	Guyana Defence Force
HE	His Excellency
HF	Home Forces
HMG	Her Majesty's Government
IB	Intelligence Bureau
Interpol	International Criminal Police Commission
IRA	Irish Republican Army
IS	Intelligence Staff
KAR	King's African Rifles

KY	Kabaka Yekka
MEA	Middle East Airlines
MI5	Security Intelligence
MI6	Secret Intelligence Service
MIA	Ministry of Internal Affairs
M.o.D	Ministry of Defence
MV	motor vessel
NCO	non-commissioned officer
NRR	Northern Rhodesian Regiment
NSDAP	Nationalsozialistische Deutsche Arbeiterpartei (National Socialist German Worker's Party/Nazi Party)
NSW	New South Wales
ODA	Overseas Development Administration
ODM	Ministry of Overseas Development
OTC	Officers' Training Corps
P&O	Pacific and Orient
PAFMECA	Pan-African Freedom Movement in East and Central Africa
PC	provincial commissioner
PS	Permanent Secretary
PWD	Public Works Department
RAF	Royal Air Force
RMS	Royal Mail Steamer
RN	Royal Navy
RT	radio-telegraphy
SA	Sturm Abteilung (Brown Shirts)
SAS	Special Air Service
SS	steamship
TANU	Tanganyika National Union
UK	United Kingdom
UKLF	United Kingdom Land Forces
UNM	Uganda National Movement
UPC	Uganda People's Congress
USIS	United States Information Service
VCO	Viceroy's Commissioned Officer
YAR	Yemen Arab Republic

Glossary

abawajjere	common man
amah	nanny
Arbeitsdienst	work service
askari	policeman, soldier or guard
Auslandsamt der Deutschen Berufsgruppen	Foreign Office of German Professional Groups
baraza	open meeting
Bund	waterfront or association
bwana	Mr, master
chumba cha maiti	room of the corpses
consolata	Italian consul
Daibutsu	Buddha
Deutsche Angestelltenschaft	German Employees' Union
Deutscher Handlungsgehilfen-verband	German Commercial Assistants' Union
Deutsche Nationalpartei	German National Party
effendi	officer (Arabic)
Fichte Bund	propaganda press
Gauleiter	district leader
gombolola	parish
Hakenkreuz	swastika
imam	Muslim priest
inyenzi	cockroach
jambia	dagger
Kassenwart	treasurer (of each *Ortsgruppe* and *Stützpunkt*)
khat	a shrub (*Catha edulis*), whose

	leaves are chewed for their stimulant effect
kondo	robber
Kreis	provincial leader
Kriminalamt	CID
Landesgruppe	headquarters in territory
Landesgruppenleiter	leader in territory
Luftwaffe	German air force
Lukiiko	Buganda Parliament
mailo	system of land tenure
manyatta	stockade (Masai)
matoke	plantain
mazbut	Turkish coffee
memsahib	term of respect for a European married woman
Mwami	King of Rwanda
ngoma	dance
Ortsgruppenleiter	district leader
Ortsgruppe	district group
palais	palace
Regierungsrat	adviser
Reich	German State and Commonwealth
Reichstatthalter	Governor
rial	North Yemen currency
saza	county
Schriftwart	secretary
Schutzstaffel	Nazi élite corps
Schutztruppen	defence force
Serkali	authority/government
souk	market
Sturmabteilung	Brown shirts
Stützpunkt	rallying point or small group
Stützpunktleiter	local leader
Taipan	wealthy commercial families
uhuru	national independence/freedom
Wehrmacht	German armed forces

Acknowledgements

I am deeply indebited to Anthony Kirk-Greene, Lecturer in the Modern History of Africa and Fellow of St Antony's College, Oxford for his guidance and encouragement in compiling this record, to Mrs Elspeth Huxley for her continuing interest in its progress, to Mrs Diana Thomson for her painstaking and patient task of assembling the manuscript into a cohesive and presentable form and, finally, to Dr Lester Crook of I.B.Tauris and Company for his assistance in publication.

Foreword
Roy T. M. Henry CBE, MVO, QPM

This is an extraordinary account of the working life of a remarkable man, Michael Macoun, CMG, OBE, QPM, CPM, OStJ. Extraordinary because it is the chronicle of a man who spent his adult life in an exciting profession which has now become defunct — a police officer in the vanished British colonial service. Remarkable because that is the only way you can describe the character and personality of Macoun.

Those readers who are not old enough to have experienced the British colonial era will perhaps be surprised to learn that policing in the colonial empire was a service disconnected from the police forces of the United Kingdom; one joined the colonial police and was appointed by the Secretary of State for the Colonies for service in a particular territory but was liable for transfer anywhere overseas within the empire. Those who can recall that period will find the historical details of special interest, particularly those of Uganda, Tanganyika and Anguilla, whilst central African affairs dominate the principal theme of the autobiography.

The personality of Macoun shines through his writing. Although modestly he does not so claim, it is clear that he was dedicated to his calling, not only in the sense of service to 'King and Country' — although such a sentiment was never in doubt — but in the way in which he regarded his responsibilities, particularly towards his juniors. He is of gregarious nature with a ready turn of wit and humour which complements a deep understanding of the needs of others — especially his subordinates. It is unwittingly easy for him to inspire and lead, and to instil such qualities in others. This is amply illustrated in the account of the six-year Uganda turmoil when he was Inspector General of the Uganda Police, a force which at that time acquitted itself admirably.

This story is made all the more interesting by the accounts and descriptions of the many personalities encountered including world leaders, royalty and a variety of others varying from Rita Hayworth and Louis Armstrong to Adolf Hitler and Idi Amin!

Although the main portion of this autobiography is of Uganda — 'The Pearl of Africa' — both the earlier years and the final period of his career make fascinating reading. He was aided in his duties by his engaging wife, Geraldine, who, through her natural sympathy and understanding of the people with whom Michael dealt, was of great assistance. His post-retirement experience was as the Inspector General of Colonial Police and Overseas Police Adviser at the Foreign and Commonwealth Office, a worldwide sphere of responsibilities, which was a fitting climax to the career of this remarkable man.

March 1996

Introduction:
The Evolution of the Police
Services in Commonwealth Africa

On the basis of 25 years' police experience of East Africa, both before and after independence, first as a member of the directing staff of the National Police Staff College in Britain and then, for 13 years until my retirement, as the Secretary of State's senior overseas police adviser in his Foreign and Commonwealth Office (FCO), this introduction spans four decades and, for presentational purposes, is divided into three periods — the colonial era, the period of decolonization from the end of the Second World War and the aftermath of independence.

* * *

The colonial police service was constituted in 1936 as part of a plan to unify the colonial service, which was inaugurated in 1930. It was not a centrally controlled service, but it provided an opportunity for interterritorial transfer of gazetted (or commissioned) officers appointed by the Secretary of State for the Colonies. In practice, this seldom took place in the colonial era except in the more senior ranks. The pattern of service in British Africa was within regional groupings — East, central, West and southern.

It may with some justification be said that in the immediate prewar period, when I first joined the colonial police service, after a year's training with the Metropolitan Police, the police forces in

British Africa bore little resemblance to the police service in the UK. Most forces were established on the model of the Royal Irish Constabulary and were essentially paramilitary in character.

As accurately described in Sir Charles Jeffries's book on the colonial police, 'they were organized mainly with a view to the suppression of crimes of violence and mass outbreaks against the peace.' This is a far cry from the traditional concept of the role of the police in this country. In 1939, at the outbreak of the war, all the police forces in British Africa were capable of being mobilized as defence support units. Many of them saw active service and provided gendarmerie units to police occupied enemy territories.

The nature of these forces was clearly reflected in their officer cadres. For instance, on arrival in East Africa as a cadet officer with a year's training with the Metropolitan Police behind me, I was surprised to find that many of the senior officers had had no formal police training and, in some cases, no practical operational experience. The training school, which was referred to as the depot, was under the command of a former Guards regimental sergeant major. Training was almost entirely confined to basic discipline, drill, weapon training and field exercises. The delegation of responsibility to African officers stopped at the rank of sergeant major and all executive posts were held by British expatriate officers, both gazetted and inspectorate with a leavening of Asian inspectors, largely engaged in prosecution, clerical, stores and technical duties.

Crime of a serious nature was invariably investigated by an expatriate officer, and lesser offences, outside the main centres of population, were left to the local or tribal authorities. Due to the relatively small number of expatriate gazetted officers (there were only 1500 in all in the whole colonial police service) all but those units based in the main towns came under the direction and control of the provincial administration and, in most upcountry districts, the officer in charge of police was the district commissioner, who was a general factotum responsible for administration as well as magisterial and police duties. This could hardly be considered conducive to the development of a professional police service, least of all for local African officers.

The outbreak of war emphasized the secondary defence role of the police. In Tanganyika, where I was serving at the time, there was the problem of rounding up and interning the substantial German population, and at the same time keeping a close watch on subversion. As Tanganyika was an ex-German colony, certain elements in the African population remained pro-German. This gave rise to a spate of rumours of espionage and subversion. By 1940 and the entry of Italy into the war there were real reasons for anxiety, for East Africa was only lightly defended and if the Italian armies in Ethiopia and Somaliland had had the will to invade, it was seriously believed that they could have overrun much of Kenya and parts of northeast Uganda.

The defection of Madagascar to Vichy France and the German submarine war in the Indian Ocean and the Mozambique channel brought new dimensions of war and threats to British East Africa. However, internal peace prevailed in most if not all of British Africa and crime rates remained low. Many expatriate police officers were seconded for military duties as a result of which supervision of law enforcement forces was even more scanty. With the end of the war, a totally new situation had arisen and previous attitudes had to be radically changed and new policies formulated.

✻ ✻ ✻

Tens of thousands of African ex-servicemen returned to their homelands with experience of the Middle East, Southeast Asia and the Mediterranean, and with limited prospects of resettlement. Africans were no longer prepared to accept a role of perpetual subordination and there was at the same time a drift to the towns. Crime, strikes and civil disorder increased and it was necessary to revise attitudes not only to the role and functions of the police service but also to the future training of local officers to accept and exercise responsibility.

Senior officers with previous experience in the West Indies, Southeast Asia and Palestine were transferred to British African colonies, where they injected a greater degree of professionalism and a fresh philosophy into the problems of law enforcement. A more enlightened approach to the training and welfare of African officers resulted in marked progress in the provision of genuine police training facilities, tolerable levels of housing accommodation and a progressive if tardy delegation of duties to indigenous officers.

The key to the delegation of duties to local officers lay in basic educational standards and effective and relevant police as opposed to paramilitary training. No longer were Africans recruited solely for their physiques and unquestioning obedience to the discipline of the regimental depot. Conditions of pay and service had to be improved to encourage better educated school leavers to join the police rather than the more popular and less demanding white collar jobs in the private sector. This essential and belated change of direction depended largely on the leadership of the police forces in Africa and fortunately a new generation of enlightened and professional police commissioners emerged.

It was at the same time necessary not to lose the paramilitary capability of the police forces to meet the increase in civil disorder, violent strikes and a succession of minor revolts followed by major rebellions such as Mau Mau and widespread rioting in Nyasaland, Northern Rhodesia and Uganda. Thus, concurrently with the development of professional police forces capable of dealing with crime prevention, investigation of serious crime, traffic control in major urban areas and many other civil police duties, it was vital to ensure that all forces had a built-in internal security capability.

This involved a marked improvement in security intelligence (Special Branch) services and the creation of riot control and internal security field forces. The latter were known variously as general service units, special forces, police mobile forces or units, motorized companies or field forces.

In essence, they were all similar in composition, role and equipment. They had mobility and both a riot control and field operational capability. In most police forces the personnel of these specialized paramilitary units were interchangeable with the main forces and were all initially trained and enjoyed the status of police officers. By a system of biennial rotation, it was progressively possible to ensure over the years that every able-bodied man in the police forces of Africa was not only trained but experienced in internal security duties.

There were exceptions to this principle of retention of police identity and interchangeability and, in those forces that did not follow it, paramilitary forces either had an inferior standard of intake or became an elite corps, divorced from the civil police.

In the run-up to independence, with notable but few exceptions, the task of law enforcement and maintaining civil order became a formidable task. Police forces had to be substantially increased and re-equipped, and conditions of service had to be improved to ensure that the main linchpin of effective civil administration remained loyal and contented.

Disorders — industrial, civil, political and intertribal — were frequent and the police forces in British Africa had to be trained and equipped to respond promptly, efficiently and professionally. This involved a high degree of restraint and, apart from a few well-publicized occasions where the police overreacted, it can be said that on the whole the forces in British Africa conducted themselves honourably and responsibly.

In the midst of all this pre-independence turmoil, which had to be contained, there was a pressing need to pursue a phased and progressive programme of localization of command posts in these colonial forces so that by independence the community could be seen to be policed by its own indigenous officers. There was also a much greater degree of consultation with local communities and development of police–public relations.

There did not appear to be any common approach to this problem and, speaking personally, I feel that a good deal more guidance in this respect could have been given by the Colonial Office in London. The late Sir Andrew Cohen, one of the last governors of Uganda, stated that 'the only effective training in responsibility is the genuine exercise of responsibility.' Trite perhaps, but to the point.

In West Africa, due to higher educational standards, the programme of localization was undertaken well in advance of independence. In Kenya and Northern Rhodesia, where an expatriate inspectorate was retained, progress was slow, only to be further retarded in Kenya by the onslaught of the Mau Mau, where the police force had to be more than doubled at short notice. In Tanganyika, the appointment of African gazetted officers had been accepted a few years before independence, but there were far too few by 1961 and the inevitable post-independence reaction was the arbitrary termination of expatriate contracts at short notice and the promotion of inexperienced and untried African officers. In Uganda, despite an almost constant state of disorder in the years preceding independence in 1962 (between 1959 and 1964 while I was inspector-general of police in Uganda we had no less than 27 emergencies ranging from a trade boycott of Asians, accompanied by riots and bombings, to intertribal and anti-government revolts and an army mutiny), a target was set once the likely date of independence was known to ensure that, by independence day, all executive posts of command in the districts were filled by trained and experienced African officers. This was only possible by the introduction in 1960 (following the lead by Nigeria) of a command training programme in the UK (conducted at the West Yorkshire Police Academy in Wakefield) to which potential district commanders were sent. By independence day no less than 110 Ugandan officers had successfully completed this training. This programme of command training was subsequently adopted in Malawi, Tanzania, Botswana, Lesotho and Swaziland, albeit after independence.

With pre-independence localization of command posts, it was also necessary to retain those expatriate officers filling senior administrative and specialized posts who could not be speedily localized to ensure the maintenance of standards of professionalism essential in a rapidly developing society. Here again, in the absence of central direction from London, there were marked variations of approach to the problem.

Thus, as most of British Africa moved towards independence, the challenges and changes in attitudes increased and the police services were put to their most severe tests in maintaining civil order in an ever more turbulent continent as well as preparing their African colleagues to take over their responsibilities. The speed of decolonization, when it came, created stresses and difficulties never before imagined or experienced and it is to the credit of the British police service in Africa that standards of professionalism, honesty and impartiality were generally maintained.

* * *

The Evolution of the Police Services in Commonwealth Africa

In 1950, there were no less than 14 British-administered police forces in Africa: by 1970 there were none. In 1948, the Secretary of State for the Colonies had decided to appoint a police adviser to be available for consultation with colonial governments as well as advising him on overseas police matters. Although the police adviser, who was subsequently redesignated inspector-general of colonial police, to enable him to carry out inspections of overseas forces, had no executive authority and served in a purely civilian capacity, he was able to provide professional advice, coordinate training programmes in the UK for overseas officers and generally to act as a reference point in Whitehall. The post has been maintained ever since and I personally had the privilege of holding it from 1966 until the end of 1979. By then the inspectoral role, rather naturally, was confined to the remaining dependent territories.

It was clear that in the immediate post-independence period there was a continuing need for independent commonwealth police forces to be provided with advice, training and assistance from London and a wise decision was made with the merger of the Commonwealth Relations Office (CRO) and Colonial Office in 1966 and again with the establishment of the FCO in 1967 to preserve this small department in Whitehall to act as a central point for all overseas police matters in which Her Majesty's Government had an interest.

The measure of that assistance can best be assessed in the number of consultancy visits carried out by my deputy and myself in the years 1966–79. These totalled 68 and covered no less than 17 commonwealth countries in Africa; in addition there were many more to other parts of the world. They also included non-commonwealth countries in Africa such as Ethiopia, Mali and Senegal. Consultancy visits to independent commonwealth countries in Africa were carried out in response to requests for advice and organization, operational techniques, equipment and training by the governments concerned and, as often as not, linked with British development aid and technical cooperation programmes. The Overseas Development Administration (ODA) had given generous and consistent aid in this respect over the period under review.

Introduction

Although police development did not necessarily feature as a high priority in the philosophy of development aid, its essential role within the framework of government was recognized and assistance was forthcoming where it could be shown that it was to be used to help the developing world to help itself. Aid had therefore primarily been in the direction of technical cooperation, either by providing British support and in-service training officers, or by ensuring that requests for training in the UK in management and specialized skills were met.

In 1979 there were still six British advisory or training missions in the independent commonwealth countries in Africa, as well as some 40 British police officers serving under direct contracts with host countries. In addition, 765 police officers from former British Africa had undergone training in the UK since 1970.

Specially designed staff training, instructor and detective courses had been organized to meet the requirements of overseas police forces and at least seven different UK police training establishments readily participated in providing both the instructional staff and the accommodation to ensure the fulfilment of this programme. There can be few senior officers in the commonwealth countries in Africa who have not had the benefit of this professional training in the UK. At the same time, the FCO has sponsored a number of work study visits by senior officers from African forces to the UK. Because of the regular inflow of overseas police officers at British police training establishments, there was full-time supervisory staff, financed by the ODA, at the National Police Staff College, Bramshill, the Metropolitan Police Training School, Hendon, and at the West Yorkshire Police Academy, Wakefield.

When funds permitted, individual members of the supervisory staff carried out course benefit tours to those regions of Africa from which trainees originated. Tours of this nature were carried out to East, central and West Africa. Thus local problems were better appreciated and contact maintained with former students. At any given time there were approximately 100 overseas police officers under instruction in the UK; more than half from former British Africa.

From the foregoing, it will be appreciated that, despite decolonization, the links were maintained and strengthened between the British police service and the police forces of erstwhile British Africa. It is relevant to observe, in this context, that professionalism rather than close political affinities undoubtedly was the major binding factor. This natural and continuing association has been greatly facilitated by the fact that, in most of the independent commonwealth countries in Africa, legal and judicial systems as well as police organization and procedures have been based on the English model.

The problems of law enforcement in former British Africa had become much more acute since the colonial era and, without the assurance that assistance in terms of reinforcement and material support were readily available from the administering power, all independent commonwealth countries in Africa had to develop a much greater degree of self reliance than in the pre-independence era. This resulted in a substantial expansion in manpower and a greater emphasis on the internal security role of the police service.

Britain has played a major part in ensuring that advice, assistance and training facilities were readily available to meet the increased commitments of civil policing; paramilitary training was excluded from our overseas development aid programmes, though some assistance in this respect was provided under the UK military training assistance scheme where members of paramilitary forces as well as those of local defence forces obtained training at service establishments in the UK.

In conclusion, it may be said, with some justification, that the legacy of British methods of law enforcement and the philosophy of a police force acting primarily in a civil role, accountable to the community as a whole, were preserved in all those countries in Africa formerly under British administration. The fact that in some of those countries the police service had been subordinated either to political or military pressures has not yet destroyed the identity and impartiality of the police service. It is worth recording that, to date, there have been no coups in former British Africa in which the police service has been directly involved. To that extent, it may be hoped that it will provide a residual influence for the continuity of civil order and a check against the abuse of political power.

1
Childhood Days in China

I was born on 27 November 1914 in Hongkew Hospital in the
international settlement in Shanghai, China. My father at that
time was commissioner of the imperial Chinese customs service in Nanking, up the Yangtze River, where we lived until 1919.
We occupied a palatial house with spacious grounds. My brother
and sister (twins) were born in Nanking in 1917.

My early recollections of Nanking were of a cosseted life with a
large staff of servants, two *amah*s (nannies), and no shortages.
During the hot weather, my mother, accompanied by us children,
would retreat to a hotel in the hills of Kuching. At home in
Nanking, we were left largely to the mercy and care of our *amah*s
and the male servants. By the age of 5 I had already learned the
mysteries of poker from the servants and to speak basic Mandarin.

* * *

In 1919 we sailed in the Lloyd Triestino liner, *Pilsener*, on postwar leave from Shanghai. We travelled via Hong Kong, Singapore,
Penang, Aden, Massawa (Eritrea), the Suez Canal, Zante (Dodecanese islands) and Brindisi to Venice, where we disembarked. We
spent a few days in the Royal Danieli Hotel, adjacent to the Piazza
San Marco, before travelling on to Paris by train. *En route*, we
witnessed a demonstration on Milan station, led by none other
than Benito Mussolini, a street agitator in those days. Later, our
train journey was interrupted by a strike and we were obliged to

stay overnight in makeshift accommodation on the Swiss side of the Simplon tunnel. There followed some blissful spring days in Paris before eventually landing in England and thence to my grandmother's house and postwar 'troubles' in Northern Ireland. We lived half way between the Malone and Lisburn roads and heard gunfire most nights. An early casualty was the nephew of my grandmother's cook, who was shot dead one night by the police (or perhaps the Black and Tans) for curfew breaking.

❊ ❊ ❊

When my father's leave ended we all set sail for China, this time on the P&O liner *Devanha*, which went via the Mediterranean, Suez, Aden and Singapore to Hong Kong, where we disembarked, hoping to obtain onward transport in a coastal ship for Amoy on the south China coast where my father had been transferred as commissioner of customs. However, on arrival in Hong Kong, we were confronted by a general strike and, as a result, spent the next two weeks in a hotel at mid-level on the Peak on Hong Kong Island. As there was no service, the *memsahib*s were obliged to take over the cleaning and cooking as well as coping with their families. Eventually, we set sail for Amoy on a coaster with an armed police guard — shipping on the coast was vulnerable to attack by pirates, assisted by infiltrators among the deck passengers who, of necessity, were penned in on the fore and aft decks behind metal cages. On arrival in Amoy we were transferred by a customs launch to Kulangsu Island, the international settlement, where our house was situated.

❊ ❊ ❊

Again, as in Nanking, this was a large manorial building, set in spacious gardens on a headland overlooking the open sea. We had the usual retinue of servants, *amah*s and an English governess (Miss Cottingham) who had travelled out from England with us. Her main function appeared to be to teach me (aged five and a half) the rudiments of English and geography. She was basically underemployed, but was in great demand by the expatriate

2

bachelor community on the island, which even at that relatively early age I found fascinating.

The expatriate community in the international settlement was socially independent and, apart from the wealthy Taipan commercial families, had very little contact with the Chinese. It needs to be said that this was not a conventional British colonial society, for the expatriate community was essentially multinational (British, American, French, Italian, Portuguese and Japanese). For example, my father's deputy commissioner of customs (Loureiro) was Portuguese and all participating nations in the treaty ports were represented on his staff.

With the abundance of social engagements and sporting activities available on Kulangsu, the expatriates would avoid going to Amoy city on the mainland unless they had to attend to official or commercial business. Celebrations of Christmas and other expatriate national and 'tribal' occasions took place at the Island Club. I have a vivid memory of being taught to dance an Irish jig, which, properly kilted and kitted out for the occasion by my mother, I performed for the assembled club members on St Patrick's Day.

Meanwhile, one was conscious, even at an early age, of events around us. One of the duties of the customs service was to search for, seize and destroy opium, the possession of which was illegal. On one occasion I was allowed to travel on the customs patrol boat while, after sailing into the Formosa Strait, the crew dumped hundreds of pounds of opium overboard. However, I noticed that some of the crew were careful to scrape off and secrete residue of opium from the deck or even from the soles of their boots. This too, the period in the early 1920s, was when China was torn by civil war. Warlords, with their private armies, fought over territory and, on one occasion, when the provincial warlord was defending his territory from a naval warlord's invading fleet, we found ourselves on Kulangsu Island in the crossfire. My mother shepherded the family and servants into the cellars of our house while shells from both sides whistled over the roof. The next day, one of our *amah*s took us three children down to the neighbouring beach to view the dead sailors who had been washed up by the incoming tide.

We remained in Amoy until early 1924 and, before we left for my father's home leave, experienced the edge of the notorious typhoon that was to sweep up the China Sea and devastate southern Japan.

Before transhipment to an ocean liner, which we were to join in Shanghai, we again travelled up the Formosa Strait on a coaster, calling in *en route* at the port of Ningpo. As we sailed from Shanghai, bound for Japan, Canada and home to Ireland, I vividly remember the skyline of imposing buildings and the *Bund* (waterfront) — the Cathay Hotel, the Hong Kong and Shanghai Bank, the Customs House (my father's old office in the early days), the Jardine Matheson buildings and others.[1] From Shanghai we sailed via Nagasaki and Kobe to Yokohama in Japan, from where we had first-hand views of the typhoon and earthquake damage earlier in the year. There were few buildings left standing in Tokyo and the quay at Yokohama had been contorted into an undulating switchback. While in Yokohama we managed to visit the famous *Daibutsu* (Buddha) at Kamakura and had a day at Hakone at the foot of Mount Fuji (Fuji-san).[2]

From Japan we sailed across the Pacific to Vancouver BC; we then enjoyed a two-week stopover at Banff, Alberta, where we had relatives, before travelling by Canadian-Pacific across the breadth of Canada to Montreal and Quebec. We met several relatives of my father's there and in Toronto, and even squeezed in a visit to Niagara Falls (where a second cousin of ours was employed on the hydroelectric scheme). Eventually, after leisurely progress through Canada, we sailed from Quebec across the Atlantic to England — and, for me, boarding school.

Thus, by the age of 10 without any formal education, I had already circumvented the world one and a half times.

---

1. They were still there, with different occupants, when my wife and I sailed up the Whangpo River on a tour of mainland China 57 years later in 1981. We stayed in what had been the Cathay Hotel (now the Ho Pin (Peace) Hotel) and I managed, with the aid of our Chinese guide, to locate the hospital building in which I was born, now a community centre where we were entertained by banner-waving children.

2. My wife and I visited Hakone many years later (1964) on our return journey round the world from Africa–Australia–Thailand–Hong Kong and Japan to the United States and the UK.

2
Student Days: 1929–38

After emerging unscathed from my preparatory school, unlike many of my contemporaries, I spent four years at Stowe (1929–33), which I remembered as halcyon days. With the sympathetic support of several of my seniors, I survived the impact of being a new boy and settled in to the largely monastic setting of a relatively isolated school in the north Buckinghamshire countryside — apart from the house matron and domestic staff, there was a total absence of female company. I applied myself to my studies and became involved in sport and other extracurricular activities, including the OTC, the debating society and the Vitruvians (a historical and architectural study group). In my last two years at Stowe, I progressed in the disciplinary structure of the school from house 'monitor' to prefect, head of house and, finally, in my last two terms, head of school, during which I struck up a close and personal rapport with our legendary headmaster, J. F. Roxburgh. Little did I realize that, in many ways, this was to be an invaluable apprenticeship for my later career in life.

Academically, once I had surmounted the hurdles of the School and Higher Certificate examinations, I graduated to the history sixth form, which prepared me for a university career at Oxford. My tutor was an eccentric but brilliant Irishman called Martin Macloughlin, who boasted more Oxford and Cambridge scholarship pupils than any other faculty. Although my efforts to obtain one were unsuccessful, my papers, taken at Oxford, exempted me from taking an entrance examination and, after an intensive and searching interview, I was accepted by University College, Oxford in the autumn of 1933. I emerged in 1936 with a modest honours degree in modern history, incorporating a thesis on American history and a reasonable proficiency in both the German and French languages.

* * *

I left Stowe in the spring of 1933 and, prior to the commencement of my university studies, spent several months as a language student in Munich, Bavaria. Here I stayed with the family of a senior functionary in the Bavarian state administration, Freiherr Paul von Stengel, who was a staunch supporter of the Bavarian *Volkspartei*. He held the post of *Regierungsrat* (adviser) on Czech affairs and could best be described as a conservative nationalist.

In the late spring of 1933, Munich was at the heart of the newly elected NSDAP (National Socialist Workers Party) and only two months previously Adolf Hitler had assumed power. This new-found German 'identity' was exemplified by vast rallies of Nazi supporters (up to 250,000), which, led prominently by the Sturm-abteilung (SA) (Brown Shirts), of whom large numbers were 'reformed' communists, took place every weekend. The new 'creed' permeated all sectors of the community, including the trade unions, replaced by the *Arbeitsdienst* (work service) cadres; the schools, in which the boys were dragooned into the Hitler Youth and the girls into the Bund Deutscher Mädeln; and the public service. In all these organizations the wearing of the *Hakenkruz* (swastika) lapel badge indicated allegiance to the new authority. Paul von Stengel rebelled against this, but eventually (two years later) succumbed to the order for fear of losing his job.

I had weekly German language and literature classes with an elderly retired teacher, Frau Kraft. She was very demanding in attention and results, but it is to her that I owe my proficiency in the language. Her family were opera enthusiasts, so I regularly, albeit reluctantly and without enthusiasm, accompanied them to performances of Wagner and Mozart operas.

One bizarre episode during this period sticks in my memory.

There were several other British and American language students in Munich at the time whom I used to meet at parties. Lord Redesdale's daughter, Unity Mitford, who had already attracted considerable notoriety for her contacts with the hierarchy at the Brown House, the headquarters of the Nazi movement in Munich, was among those who attended these parties. On one such occasion she approached three of us, Michael Grotrian (later a journalist with the *Yorkshire Post*), Patsy Delahunty (daughter of the director of the Metropolitan Opera House in New York) and myself, and asked us if we would like to meet Hitler. Despite our ambivalence to such an idea, we concurred and, several days later, met Unity by arrangement at the Osteria Bavaria restaurant in the Schellingstrasse. Hitler, accompanied by Hess, Bruckner, the infamous Streicher, and other members of the Nazi hierarchy, arrived for lunch at a table opposite ours and, after lunch, Unity duly presented us to the Führer — we had agreed among ourselves *not* give him the Nazi salute but to bow, in appropriate courteous eighteenth-century manner, instead. We were described to him as Anglo-American students, to which he retorted that he was pleased to see the Anglo-Saxon young visiting his new Reich, whereupon we withdrew and resumed drinking coffee until he and his entourage departed.

While a paying guest at the Stengels I also, on one occasion, met the *Reichstatthalter* (governor) of Bavaria, Ritter von Epp, an old-style German general who made no secret of his dislike of the new upstart Nazi government. He did not hold his post for long. Another of the Stengels' house guests was the papal nuncio, later to become Pope. Also on this first visit to Germany as a student, I made friends with a young German (Aryan) medical student from Oberstdorf in the Bavarian Alps called Alex Klopf. We used to meet from time to time at the Hofbräuhaus beer hall and on one occasion sat at the same table as a group of young officers of the SS (*Schutzstaffel*) *Deutschland Standarte*, the Nazi elite corps, all university graduates drawn from the upper crust of Munich society. Although Alex had refused to join the NSDAP, they were friendly and apparently accepted him, but alas, two weeks' later, Alex disappeared and was never seen again. I feared that his association with a foreigner and the fact that he was obviously *not* a party supporter had probably ensured that he had ended up as a 'political dissident' at Dachau concentration camp near Munich.

* * *

I returned to Munich twice between 1933 and 1937; first to meet old friends and to traverse the Alps with one of them on foot from Kufstein to Lienz via the Grossglockner; and again during an Oxford vacation in early 1937 for a three-month diploma course in German language and literature at Munich University. This was followed by a study stint in Paris during the period of Léon Blum's Popular Front regime. My tutor in Paris was proud of the fact that she had just tutored Lord Louis Mountbatten in his Royal Navy French interpretership.

* * *

Having sat (and failed) the entrance examination for the foreign service in 1937, I sought employment in the export division of Rootes Ltd, the motor manufacturers in Piccadilly, where I assume I was taken on because of my foreign languages. Nine months of '9–5' immured within glass walls caused me to 'up sticks' and, one spring day in 1938, I reported to the Colonial Office seeking employment overseas. After a series of interviews, I was accepted for the colonial police as a cadet assistant superintendent and promptly informed that I had been specially selected to attend (together with five other colonial officers) a year's course at the Metropolitan Police College, Hendon, before assignment overseas, initially to Cyprus but subsequently to Tanganyika (former German East Africa), presumably in deference to my knowledge of the German language. So it was back to school and eventually, in mid-1939, to a long career overseas.

3

Prelude to a Career in the
Police Service Overseas: 1938–9

Prior to commencement of my police training, I accepted a temporary job in June 1938 with an old Hungarian friend of mine (John Vago) in his export/import/tourist agency firm in Budapest. I had first made his acquaintance in Oxford days when I had worked during the long vacation as a courier with the National Union of Students at the student games in Hungary.

We drove out through western Europe and Austria to Budapest, where I was installed as John's assistant in an office in the Commercial Bank in Pest. I enjoyed free board and lodging in an Austro-Hungarian *palais* (converted into a pension), provided with a number of social introductions, including one to a charming Romanian sculptress, and paid a handsome salary of £5 a week. My role, apart from assisting in office and tourist courier work, was to attend meetings at which my knowledge of both French and German proved useful to my employer.

After office hours (8.00–12.00 a.m. and 5.00–8.00 p.m.) I was free and acquired a detailed knowledge of Budapest and, inevitably, its nightlife. A free weekend, which coincided with the long-forgotten 'Eger incident', which led to general mobilization in Hungary, Nazi-occupied Austria and Czechoslovakia, gave me the opportunity to travel to Hegyeshalom on the border and to file a freelance report to the *Daily Mail*. The incident was so well covered by the Western press that it is doubtful whether my report ever reached the editor's desk. After this very pleasant and interesting three months' working interlude, I returned to London to prepare myself for my new career. However, my return journey to London was bizarre and deserves mention.

✳ ✳ ✳

Our outward journey to Budapest had taken us through both Salzburg and Vienna. Vago had an introduction to Max Reinhardt, the eminent film producer who, despite the Nazi occupation of Austria, still lived in a villa outside Salzburg. We were invited to lunch there and it was clear he was preparing to leave Austria and, unknown to me, had asked Vago to ensure that his valuable stamp collection was removed from the clutches of the Nazi authorities prior to his departure. Unwittingly, I became involved in a smuggling operation. In Vienna, we met some Austrian Jewish families, one of which I had already known from a previous holiday visit to Carinthia and, here again, Vago's services were in demand. Although the Nazis had given one family permission to leave the country as refugees, they were unable to remit funds to Britain for their daughter's education, so sought our assistance. The upshot of these clandestine contacts emerged during my return by train from Budapest.

I was instructed to collect a small attaché case from a Hungarian woman acquaintance at a station halt on the outskirts of Vienna and then to await a coded telegram in Salzburg. Two days later, I received a cryptic message from Basle in Switzerland to the effect that I should leave on the train bearing delegates from the Eucharistic Congress with whom we had acted as travel agents in Budapest — 'armed' with the attaché case.

I duly booked my ticket and joined other faithful pilgrims on the platform at Salzburg station and was blessed by the Catholic hierarchy before joining the train. I positioned myself in a compartment adjacent to that of some of the more senior prelates, including Monsignor Robinson of Ireland, made friends with the travelling Nazi railway guard, plied him judiciously with bottles of beer and when, shortly before the Austro-Swiss border, the delegates vacated their compartment for lunch, slipped the anonymous attaché case into their luggage rack — trusting to the diplomatic immunity which the international delegates enjoyed. Prior to arrival in Basle, this time when the prelates were enjoying their evening meal, I retrieved the case.

On arrival in Basle, I was met by my Hungarian friend and we travelled unscathed via Calais and Dover to London. It was only after my return to England that I learned that the case had contained Reinhardt's stamp collection, 150 gold Austrian 100-schilling coins (for the Austrian Jewish girl's educational fees) and a number of unidentified passports. My 'reward' for acting as an unwitting and rather naïve courier was one of the 100-schilling coins, which I sold for ready cash of £7.50. Until the coin was sold some months later to a collector, it was displayed in the window of a shop in the Haymarket as a reminder of a youthful escapade.

* * *

Early in September 1938, after a brief holiday with friends in the Basque region of France, during which we made an abortive excursion on foot into Franco-dominated Spain but were intercepted and returned to France, I joined the junior station inspectors' course at the Metropolitan Police College at Hendon. My overseas colleagues on the course were drawn from India, Ceylon, Nigeria, the Gold Coast, Cyprus, Hong Kong and, in my case, Tanganyika. Over 50 per cent eventually attained commissioner or deputy commissioner rank in their respective countries and territories.

Initially, upon completion of the course I was destined for Cyprus and had been instructed by the Colonial Office to learn Turkish in my spare time; however, on discovering that I had completed an external diploma course in German language and literature at Munich University during my Oxford vacations, I was reassigned to Tanganyika (former German East Africa).

I spent a very happy and intensive ten months at Hendon during which all junior station inspectors were seconded to divisions in the Metropolitan Police, were attached to the immigration department and passport office and participated in operational duties (including night patrols during the upsurge of IRA activity in

11

London in 1939), as well as fulfilling a rigorous training course at the college and participating in all sporting activities, where our competitors included Sandhurst, Woolwich and Cranwell service colleges (there were only 45 of us), and completed the programme in the late summer of 1939. Many lifelong friends both in the UK police service and overseas were made and preserved for the rest of my career.

4

Introduction to Africa: 1939

Having successfully completed my training at Hendon, I left in the last few days of August 1939, travelling first to Paris with my parents and then on to Marseilles to join my ship for East Africa (the SS *Mantola* of the British India Line). Mobilization for war had already commenced in France and Paris was in turmoil; the railway termini were swarming with troops and it was clear that war was imminent.

The night before I left, I paid a farewell visit to Harry's Bar in the Rue Daunou — a favourite haunt from student days in Paris. I was not to visit it again for 26 years. The ship that was to take me on the first leg of a 25-year career in East Africa awaited us in Marseilles. The SS *Mantola* was one of the old prewar British India 'workhorses' of a 'Slow Boat to China' stamp.

The passengers included colonial service officers and their wives, businessmen and 'settlers' from East and central Africa, British army officers on secondment to East and central African regiments (KAR and NRR), a high-powered Zionist delegation, including Chaim Weizmann and Ben-Gurion, and a lone young Arab businessman from Bahrain, Hussein Yateem. The last named appeared to be ostracized by the other passengers so I deliberately struck up an acquaintanceship with him and we became good friends. He was on his way back to Bahrain via Aden from the World Fair in Chicago. He eventually became one of the best-known businessmen in Bahrain. The journey out to East Africa was punctuated with a number of incidents.

13

As stated above, war was imminent and, after a brief stopover in Malta, we were 'challenged' at night off the coast of Pantellaria, an island off the Libyan coast, by two Italian destroyers. After an exchange of signals, we were permitted to pass unmolested. On arrival in Alexandria, we were informed that war was only hours away and that it was uncertain whether the Italians would enter it in support of Hitler. The already tense atmosphere was hardly improved when, on the second morning, two Italian floatplanes flew over the harbour at low level. However, we sailed into Port Said, where we arrived on the morning of 3 September 1939. We berthed and were told that it was uncertain when we would proceed southwards through the Suez Canal. At about midday we learned that war had been declared against Germany. Coincidentally, we spotted a Royal Navy troop carrier, the SS *Dilwara*, so a group of us, mostly army and police officers, 'gatecrashed' the ship and were cordially and generously entertained by the Royal Navy to a chain of pink gins. On leaving the *Dilwara*, we noticed that a dockside office displayed a German swastika flag from a second-floor window, so, fortified with navy gin, we scaled the outside of the building and removed and destroyed the flag. The Egyptian police did not intervene and we felt, rather childishly, that we had struck our first blow for freedom.

The declaration of war inevitably resulted in interminable delays, but eventually we set sail through the canal for Suez, little realizing that we should be faced with further delays on arrival there. On entering Port Tewfik at the southern end of the canal, we learned that we would be delayed several days and were not permitted ashore. The ship was blacked out at night, so we all slept on deck on account of the suffocating heat and I secured a pitch in the bows where, armed with a portable radio and adequate supplies of liquor, I established a 'social centre' which proved popular with my fellow travellers. However, the tedium was insupportable and one evening an army friend (subsequently to rise to the rank of brigadier) and I decided to savour the pleasures of the French Club in Suez, which was opposite our anchorage. To get there, we had to bypass the master-at-arms and swim ashore. The few clothes we would require (trusting to French informality) were tied in a bundle to our heads and off we set. The swim ashore was uneventful and, having clothed ourselves, we spent a couple of hours cementing the *Entente cordiale*. At about 2.00 a.m., rather the worse for wear, we had to face the return journey and wisely decided to swim backstroke slowly together so as to provide mutual support in an emergency. After what seemed to be an age we reached the gangplank exhausted and hauled ourselves back on board unnoticed by anyone, including the master-at-arms, who had long deserted his post. Our companions on board were surprised and envious to learn the next day that we had taken 'French leave' the night before — an irresponsible, possibly dangerous, but enjoyable break from the boredom of the blacked-out ship.

After further delays, we eventually set sail for Port Sudan where we remained for two days, during which my army friend and I took a taxi to the derelict and ghostly port of Suakim and experienced the first mirages crossing the desert *en route*. The next port of call was Aden — a hive of activity in those days — and thence past Cape Guardafui to Mogadishu, Mombasa and finally to my destination, Dar es Salaam.

Having never been in East Africa before, I had little or no idea what to expect. 'Old hands' on board warned me that I was about to enter a world where heavy drinking among Europeans was the norm. As it happened I arrived on a Sunday morning, so, fortified with two stiff gins after breakfast, I was prepared for my entrée. I was met by a staff officer who was suffering from a monumental hangover and he took me to my quarters. I was initially to be billeted with the superintendent in charge of the Police Training Depot until I had been allocated a bachelor flat. On arrival, I was conducted to my host's flat to be informed that he was still in bed, also recovering from a hangover. When he eventually surfaced, I was informed that there had been a King's African Rifles (KAR) mess party the night before and that a number of army officers and their wives would be joining a 'hair of the dog' curry lunch at midday. After this introduction to service life in Dar es Salaam, nothing surprised me thereafter.

* * *

The Tanganyika Police Force in those early war days was commanded by an ex-regular army officer and most of the senior officers were either former British South Africa (Rhodesia) police or ex-army officers with limited police experience. Several were excellent and impartial administrators but there were very few with practical operational police experience.

An 'injection' early in the war of ex-Palestine police officers at least improved the professionalism of the force. Apart from another cadet assistant superintendent who had attended the Metropolitan Police College at Hendon, none had attended anything other than basic police training courses. However, as we were members of what was essentially a paramilitary force and crime levels were low, the effectiveness of the force was more than adequate to meet its commitments.

5

The War Years

O n my arrival in Dar es Salaam in September 1939, war had already been declared and, as the Italians had not entered the contest, the primary task of the British administration in Tanganyika was to round up all German enemy aliens. As I was a German speaker and had recently spent some time in Germany studying for my diploma in German language and literature, I was a 'natural' for posting to Special Branch — redesignated for the war conditions as the Department of Intelligence and Security. My boss was Neil Stewart, the deputy commissioner, who was a tough extrovert Scot. The department consisted of myself as coordinator, a half-Irish, half-Danish inspector called Roland Godbey, who was fluent in German and Kiswahili, Eleanor Lewis, a linguist and South African university graduate, and supporting clerical staff.

* * *

It may not be known that over 3000 male Germans (who outnumbered the British in the private sector in the country) had to be rounded up and interned. My first tasks were to identify active Nazis within the community and, from the mass of documents seized throughout the country from Germans at the outbreak of the war, to determine the scale of prewar Nazi penetration in the country. After several months of painstaking research and numerous visits to German centres in the territory, we were able not only to arrest and detain the great majority of those who were considered a security risk but also to document a revealing record of the penetration of the community up to the outbreak of war. This was duly completed and presented to the British Administration of Tanganyika Territory some months later (see Appendices A and B).

The womenfolk and children of the detainees (who were housed in a converted PWD warehouse compound on the Pugh Road outside Dar es Salaam) were concentrated in the coffee farming area of Oldeani in the Crater Highlands of northern Tanganyika under a police commandant and supervisory staff. The majority of able-bodied German Nazis were later transhipped to detention camps in South Africa; those unfit for war service were repatriated to Germany with their families by Italian ships; the wives and families of the Nazis were transported to southern Africa and confined to camps in South Africa and Rhodesia; and the non-Nazis (mostly Jews) were permitted to remain in Tanganyika on parole. A few of the latter volunteered for war service but, as enemy aliens, could not join the British forces in the earlier stages of the war. One, however, joined the Free French forces in the Western Desert and was awarded the Croix de Guerre at Bir Hakeim.

One of those who managed to persuade the medical authorities that he was unfit for war service was due for repatriation to the 'fatherland', but on deportation was discovered to have a *Luftwaffe* intelligence officer's uniform in a false bottom to his travelling case (see Appendix B); he therefore joined his colleagues in detention in South Africa. We arranged for his uniform to be sent to Security Intelligence Middle East, Cairo and I learned later that it was put to good use by the Long Range Desert Group in its raids on Rommel's camps in the Western Desert.

* * *

Social life proceeded apace in Dar es Salaam and one was absorbed, as a bachelor of dubious eligibility, by the KAR as well as the police community. There was a small contingent of Women's Transport Service FANYs (First Aid Nursing Yeomanry) attached to the army sub-area headquarters in Dar es Salaam. The sergeant in charge was Geraldine Sladen; her parents had gone to farm in Kenya in 1919 and her brother Eddie had been at school with me at Stowe. Before long we became engaged, though I had to obtain special dispensation from my commissioner as I was still an 'unconfirmed' assistant superintendent. In November 1940 we were married in Nairobi; Geraldine was given away by her brother, who was later killed in Burma while serving with the East African forces. After a short honeymoon in Nyeri we returned to our respective posts in Dar es Salaam.

Some months later Geraldine had to obtain her discharge from the army as she was pregnant and our first-born, Brian, arrived in early October 1941 at the Ocean Road Hospital in Dar es Salaam. The acting governor's wife, Mrs Freeston, insisted she spend a few days convalescence in Government House, which was an unexpected bonus for the wife of a *very* junior gazetted police officer.

We lived in Dar es Salaam until mid-1943 when I was posted to the Combined Services Security Bureau in Nairobi, where our second son, Tony, was born in February 1944. Throughout my career in East Africa, Geraldine had consistently become involved in either a support or voluntary capacity in many activities associated with my duties, although during our early years she was mainly occupied with the children.

Apart from purging Tanganyika of the Nazi presence, our main task in security was to neutralize pro-German and anti-British elements in the African population. There were a number of ex-*askaris* from von Lettow-Vorbeck's forces in the First World War who were known to be encouraging non-cooperation with the British war effort in East Africa, principally by propaganda against joining the KAR. Once they had been identified, they were 'rusticated' to remote areas of the country under supervision for the duration.

* * *

19

Early in 1940, I was detached from Special Branch for a few months to act as assistant to the commandant of the Police Training School. The 'depot', as it was known, only aspired to training raw recruits in drill, musketry and basic police procedures. In practice, it could best be described as a paramilitary training depot. The supervisory staff consisted of an ex-guardsman as commandant, myself (newly fledged from a year's police training with the Metropolitan Police), an Irish inspector and an ex-drill sergeant-major. The orderly sergeant and NCOs were African with a background of military training and no police skills.

Our programme of training was directed to produce a paramilitary force in support of the KAR. In the event, after the collapse of the Italian forces in 1941, a substantial number of officers, NCOs and trainees were transferred to the Somalia gendarmerie in Mogadishu.

After six months of tedious depot life with endless parades, fatigues, field training, route marches and a rather pathetic project digging slit trenches around the perimeter of the barracks against the non-existent threat of an Italian attack, I was relieved to return to Special Branch and then, though still an unconfirmed assistant superintendent, to take over as director of Intelligence and Security. My predecessor departed to command the Somalia gendarmerie in occupied enemy territory in Mogadishu.

* * *

In 1941/2, although on the fringe of the war in East Africa, life was full of action and incident. Apart from providing bases for both the South African Air Force (operating Junker 87s and Avro Anson aircraft on antisubmarine patrols as far south as Mozambique Channel) and later the RAF (in long-range Catalinas) on reconnaissance flights (via Mauritius) into the south Indian Ocean, we were 'hosts', in turn, to thousands of Italian prisoners of war from Ethiopia and Somalia, to 13,000 Polish refugees from Russia via Tehran and Karachi, to 400–500 Greek refugees from the northern Dodecanese, German Jewish refugees from Cyprus, and a handful of 'white' Italians who had cooperated with the British forces during the invasion of Ethiopia and Somalia. Documentation, surveillance and identification of troublemakers in some of the above categories kept our hands full in the directorate of security and intelligence.

＊ ＊ ＊

In 1942 Polish refugees began arriving in Dar es Salaam from Russia via Tehran. Some 1000 women and children came on the first ship; they were distressingly dirty and debilitated and none spoke English. They were disembarked onto a train which took them to the old German internment camp outside the town where many local women, Geraldine among them, met and assisted them.

Unfortunately, the Royal Navy was having a mock battle in preparation for landing on Madagascar and a party of marines firing blanks 'captured' the train, not realizing it contained terrified refugees fleeing from Siberia. Later, after they had been 'deloused' and had settled in we took several lorry loads of Polish children to the beach, where in great excitement they rushed into the sea and some had to be rescued.

＊ ＊ ＊

The occupation of the former Italian colonies in the Horn of Africa freed the East African forces for their war zones. Our involvement in the prelude to the plan to invade Vichy French-held Madagascar took place in 1941 and is recorded in some detail in Appendix C. Otherwise, the bulk of military forces switched to the war against Japan in the Indian subcontinent and Burma.

Meanwhile, the threat to East Africa lay largely at sea where both German and Japanese submarine fleets were notably active. No less than 17 British merchantmen were sunk in the Mozambique Channel and we had our first experience of dealing with survivors who reached the East African coast. These ranged from boatloads of half starved and dehydrated merchant seamen to a single survivor from a sinking in the Maldives Channel — a young lad who had spent over two weeks on a floating spar until picked up by a dhow which dropped him off in a southern Tanganyika port. He was in our care for several days and I had the great pleasure in communication with his parents in Liverpool to say that their 19-year-old son was alive and well. His personality must have saved his mind; when questioned on how he fared, floating on his own in the Indian Ocean, he merely responded in good Scouse style by saying that he just twiddled his thumbs and sang songs to himself.

* * *

Late in 1942, despite regular pleas to be released for active service since late 1939 without response, I was informed that I was to be seconded to the Combined Services Security Bureau in Nairobi as the police representative with the acting rank of major. This was a curious organization, with MI5 and MI6 responsibility and with a small staff comprising a security service officer in charge and supported by an ex-inspector-general of the Indian police, an army major from IB East Africa Command and myself. We were attached to the offices of the East African Governors' Conference in Shell House, Nairobi and acted as a clearing house for all security intelligence and counterintelligence activities in the command. These included shipping intelligence, the processing of detained enemy agents and the oversight of two combined services detention and interrogation centres near Nairobi — one for Italian generals captured in the Ethiopian campaign and the other for enemy agents who fell into our hands from as far afield as Mozambique.

My family and I took up residence in the Muthaiga area of Nairobi and my attachment, which was packed with incidents, lasted for 12 months until the end of 1944 when I was recalled for police duties in Tanganyika.

* * *

My first command was as officer in charge of Iringa District in the Southern Highlands Province of Tanganyika. This was to be my first true experience of conventional police duties since my year's training at the Metropolitan Police College in Hendon in 1938/9. Iringa District had a resident African population of some 300,000 strong.

It was also the heartland of the Hehe tribe who had displayed heroic resistance to the German administration during the Maji-Maji rebellion in the first decade of the century. The site of a devastatingly successful ambush of the German *Schutztruppen* in the Irole Pass was still marked by a commemorative obelisk, and some 40 years later the older members of the tribe still remembered the tribal resistance and passing triumph against the Germans. As I later found out as the officer in charge of the police, the legend of Mkwawa's suicide had been absorbed into the tribe's traditions and mores in a rather unusual way (see below).

* * *

My command was exercised through an Asian inspector (a Sikh), an African sub-inspector (an amiable drunk), a sergeant-major and 50 other ranks. As officer in charge of police during the immediate postwar years in upcountry Tanganyika, one was exposed to the whole range of serious crime which, in those days, was largely confined to 'offences against the person'. This embraced murder, manslaughter, suicide and assault — usually involving grievous bodily harm. Burglary and housebreaking were happily rare and theft was usually of a petty nature. As the only expatriate officer in a district police unit, it was my lot not only to attend the scene of crime in all serious cases but also to investigate the offence and, in due course, prosecute in court. It was my first independent command and the experience was to stand me in good stead for the rest of my police career.

It was a requirement in Tanganyika to pass the higher standard Kiswahili language examination within the first six years of service. This qualified one to act as an interpreter, which was essential for court work, where, due to illiteracy, most proceedings required double interpretation (i.e. vernacular to Kiswahili and Kiswahili to English, the court language).

A disproportionately high number of serious cases involved

homicide, with relatively minor disputes often resolved by the use of a knife, club, machete, spear or muzzle-loading gun. In my first year of upcountry police experience I had to deal — largely single-handedly — with murders, manslaughters and assaults causing grievous bodily harm. The motives for these crimes were sometimes as trivial as a wife's failure to have a meal ready for the 'breadwinner' on his return from work (often drunk on home-made beer or spirits); there were also disputes over land or cattle, and *crimes passionelles*.

Investigation of most of these offences was simplified by the willingness of witnesses to testify and, as often as not, by the culprit's frank admission of guilt. Forensic assistance was virtually non-existent and, in establishing the cause of death, the one resident medical officer relied heavily on the police. Since this invariably necessitated attendance at postmortems, conducted in the cramped confines of an airless mortuary, it was in our mutual interest to establish the cause of death as speedily as possible.

In one case, the victim of an intertribal affray was carried, dead, for three days through the bush. He was unrecognizable as human and I was able, from enquiries, to point out to the doctor that death was due to a severed radial artery. The deceased's hands and wrists were fortunately still identifiable as human parts.

On another occasion, an African farmer ran amok after drinking an excess of home-brewed spirit, shot three wives and a daughter dead with his muzzle-loader and then blew the top of his head off. For good measure, the police truck bringing the bodies in to the district headquarters was obliged to collect yet another body of a man who had drowned in a river *en route*. There was no alternative but to lay out the bodies on the mortuary lawn and for the postmortems to be carried out perfunctorily in the open. The fact that I was able to identify the cause of death was a great relief to the medical officer and myself.

As mentioned above, tradition played an interesting role in the incidence of unnatural deaths in the district. I was somewhat surprised during the first few months of my service to be confronted with a number of suicides. These were, almost invariably, of women who were found hanging from a tree in the bush, garrotted with woven strips of bark from a tree. It transpired that the motive for suicide was apparently trivial — a family quarrel, a dispute over failing to provide a husband's meal, or a refusal to provide 'conjugal rights'.

As this appeared peculiar to the Wahehe, I endeavoured to discover whether there was some underlying reason for the phenomenon. After some research, I was told by local tribesmen that when a punitive expedition was mounted against the Wahehe after Chief Mkwawa and his warriors had inflicted a severe defeat by ambush on the German occupiers of Tanganyika in the hills to the north-east of Iringa at the beginning of the century, Mkwawa had been trapped on a hill-top and, rather than surrender to the Germans, had committed suicide by a self-inflicted wound with a muzzle-loader. According to the legend, which had lived on into the middle of the twentieth century, if a husband reviled his wife for failure of duty and said, 'You know what you must do', she would be obliged to retreat to the bush and take her life.

With a small unit and very limited professional support, it was my lot not only personally to investigate all serious crimes but also to prosecute offenders in both the district court and the stipendiary magistrate's monthly sessions. There was no jury; the bench, with two assessors (usually drawn from prominent African elders or traders), had to ensure that the defence case was adequately prosecuted. Cases involving European or Asian defendants were defended by counsel who, for the most part, were Asian lawyers. After an unsuccessful prosecution, one of the latter confessed to me that the defendant would be 'punished' in any case because he always doubled his fees for a successful defence case.

The practical experience of this isolated command, in which one had to rely on oneself for the whole range of police preventive, detective and prosecution duties, was of inestimable value and it must be said that my year's grounding at the Metropolitan Police College at Hendon in 1938/9 stood me in good stead. On many an occasion I referred to my college notes — unashamedly.

* * *

However, early in 1946, I was unexpectedly transferred to take command of the police in the whole of the Southern Highlands

Province in Mbeya with the acting rank of superintendent. My new provincial command embraced five districts including the Lupa Goldfields (administered from Chunya), Mbeya, which extended to the Northern Rhodesia border, Tukuyu, a tea-growing area with spectacular mountain scenery, adjacent to Lake Nyasa (with some of the best trout fishing in the country), Njombe to the east, in which we had a large Polish refugee camp, and Iringa, my previous district command.

From a police point of view, the principal features of the province were the Klondike-type society on the goldfields and the sophistication of the Nyakyusa (Tukuyu District) in the art of housebreaking and burglary. The latter were memorable for their choice of targets, invariably prominent people, including my commissioner who was cleaned out during an inspection visit of my headquarters' station. The Nyakyusa were adept too in the use of drug-bearing pollen, which they used to good effect on their victims. A district commissioner in Tukuyu, admittedly rather the worse for wear, woke up one morning to find himself stripped of his bedclothes and pyjamas after a raid; on another occasion, an agricultural officer on tour woke up on his camp bed one morning to find himself beside a stream some two miles from his camp.

6

Postwar and the 'Wind of Change': 1945–59

Early in 1947, I was unexpectedly transferred for a few months to take charge of the division covering the capital city of Dar es Salaam and neighbouring districts, as a substantive superintendent of police. The aftermath of the war had created new problems of urban civic and industrial unrest, fanned by the return of thousands of ex-soldiers who had tasted life outside East Africa and were finding it difficult to settle down into their old way of life. Resettlement plans were only partially effective and there was a large drifting population of dissatisfied and largely unemployed ex-soldiers.

* * *

Finally, during the year, we were granted home leave in the United Kingdom after no less than seven and a half years in East Africa. Shipping was scarce and air travel non-existent so, accompanied by my wife and our two small sons, we embarked on the *Winchester Castle* of the Union Castle Line.

Conditions on board were congested and chaotic. My wife and children shared a four-berth cabin with another police wife from Kenya with her three children, while the menfolk were banished to troopship 'standee' accommodation in the holds of the ship. Our 'dormitory' housed 169 men in tiered bunk stands. The smell and noise was just bearable but the close-packed proximity of one's companions was disturbing to say the least if not, at times, very embarrassing. I invariably woke in the morning to find that my 'mate' had thrown his arm over my face in the night and nearly stifled me. Ablutions (so-called) were communal and theft, usually by crew members, was rampant. On one occasion, my wife found the stewardess rummaging through her suitcase on a chance visit to the cabin during the morning clean-up period. There was also a lot of sickness among the children on board. Arrival in Southampton on a dark cold spring day was a relief only to be marred by the utter dreariness, cold and shortages of immediate postwar Britain.

After a relatively short leave spent visiting relatives and a brief visit to the Swiss Alps, during which we were robbed *en route* by the wagon-lit attendant in Ostend, we returned separately to East Africa — this time by different ships. My journey was entertaining, travelling with kindred spirits from East Africa; my wife's was hell, travelling with two small and adventurous, restless boys. She was congratulated on arrival in Mombasa for having completed the journey without losing them.

❊ ❊ ❊

On my return to Dar es Salaam, I was assigned to headquarters, this time as head of Special Branch. Although flattered at my promotion, I wondered if I was ever to escape from being branded as a security intelligence specialist. It took a further two years before I was able to persuade the authorities that I had joined the service as a *police* officer.

❊ ❊ ❊

At the end of 1949 we were granted our backlog of wartime accumulated leave, so we decided to take advantage of the seven and a half months due and visit Australasia and Ceylon via South Africa. Our departure on leave from Dar es Salaam could hardly have been more inauspicious given that our ship, the *Llangibby Castle* (Union Castle again), caught fire before we sailed. We were not evacuated but sat in harbour while the holds smouldered and the ventilators pumped the smoke into the staterooms and cabins for two days until the fire was brought under control. Finally, we set sail, first to Zanzibar then to Beira (the ship broke down *en route* in the Mozambique Channel), Durban and Cape Town. We needed the two weeks in the Cape to recover and then boarded the *Dominion Monarch* of the Shaw Saville Line for Australia and New Zealand.

This was the first time that we were able to enjoy the much-vaunted pleasures of travel in an ocean liner. The crossing of the southern Indian Ocean, as far south as the 'Roaring Forties', was uneventful apart from the day when our younger son, Tony, then barely 6 years old, decided to 'explore' the engine room and disappeared. There was a general alarm as it was feared he might have fallen overboard, but he was found eventually standing on a platform in the engine room mesmerized by the steady rhythm of the engines. Relief was tempered by fury on my part and he was given a good hiding with a 'light tamarind cane' (Tanganyika prison issue) when he was returned to our cabin.

Our voyage took in the ports of call of Fremantle (Perth), Melbourne and Sydney, and we eventually disembarked, after a near-hurricane in the Cook Strait in Wellington, New Zealand. Evidently, someone on board whom we had met knew of my African police experience and, shortly after arrival, I was beset by the local press and was embarrassed the next day to read of my lurid adventures as a police officer in Africa. We beat a hasty retreat, by train, to Rotorua and, after a few days staying with a New Zealand 'pen friend' family, moved on to Auckland.

Having deposited our two small sons at a nursery boarding school (vegetarian and run by two English teachers who were nudists) at Takapuna beach, north of Auckland, we spent the next two months 'exploring' both North and South islands. As petrol rationing was still in force, we were obliged to do all our travel by 'service car' (country bus) which gave one a unique insight into rural life in the islands. We covered most of both the North and South islands during the next two months, visiting Hamilton, Wellington, Christchurch, Dunedin, Queenstown (during which we walked in the mountains on day trips, including getting caught in a snowstorm), the Mount Cook area (more mountain walks, including Mt Borodino), the west coast (Hokitika and Franz Joseph glacier), Greymouth, Nelson, Picton (fishing in the Cook Strait and experiencing earth tremors before leaving), Mt Egmont (which we climbed), Rotorua (three days' superb trout fishing at Atiamuri on the Waikato River), Tongariro National Park (more mountain walks, in the snow), Auckland, Bay of Islands (Russell), and Hokianga on the northwest coast. Then, finally, we were 'at rest' for three weeks at Takapuna beach in a rented bach where we were joined by our two small boys on their 'release' from their nudist-cum-vegetarian nursery school. They both burst out in boils on resumption of a normal diet.

Our next port of call was Sydney, NSW, which we reached after a very stormy crossing of the Tasman Sea, pursued by a cyclone. We had arranged to rent an apartment at Cremorne Point, overlooking Sydney harbour and the world-famous bridge. Whilst in Sydney we travelled to Kosciusko in the Snowy Mountains for a few days' rather indifferent skiing, as well as visiting local beaches, Bondi, Manby, the Tauranga zoo and the Blue Mountains. We were fortunate in meeting and making friends with a prominent Sydney architect and his wife at Kosciusko whom we met on our return to Sydney and had a 'conducted tour' of the Sydney Opera House, then under construction.

After several weeks in Australia, we were due to move on and booked a passage to Colombo on the P&O *Mooltan*. The ship was full of young Australians bound, in most cases, for their first visit to Europe. The journey, via Melbourne, Adelaide and Perth (Fremantle), was uneventful except for the fact that both our sons developed mumps on board and had, together with other infectious children, to be corralled off in a wired-off pen on the stern of the ship. Fortunately, on arrival in Colombo help was at hand. First, the inspector-general of police, S. A. Dissanayake, who had attended the same Metropolitan Police course at Hendon as I had before the war, met us in a police patrol boat and escorted us through the health, customs and immigration formalities; also, and more importantly, a second cousin of mine, Dermot McClatchie and his wife Peggy, had invited us to stay with them for a month while awaiting a ship to take us back to East Africa.

The McClatchies (he was the manager of the Hong Kong & Shanghai Bank in Colombo) had a splendid colonial mansion in Maitland Crescent and we were installed in great comfort as their guests. They had no less than 11 servants — from a butler (Apu) to a dog servant (Podin).

While in Ceylon we were entertained in Colombo and also took trips to Kandy and Newara Eliya, as well as visiting coastal resorts in the south. During the visit to Kandy, on which I was accompanied by our elder son, my wife having been kept behind in Colombo to nurse the younger boy who was still suffering from mumps, he developed measles, which put our onward journey at risk. However, after he had recovered but was still in quarantine, I managed (with the support of our hosts) to persuade the medical officer of health to give us clean bills for both children and shortly afterwards we were on our return journey to Mombasa and East Africa on the MV *Isipingo*. We arrived 11 days later, having been away from work for seven months.

* * *

On arrival in Mombasa, I learned that my request for operational rather than specialist duties had been met and I was posted to Arusha as northern provincial police commander.

Arusha, the administrative headquarters of Northern Province, was a most pleasant station with a good climate and beautiful scenery. In 1950, with the boys both at school, Geraldine was able to become more involved with police activities. She found that most of the African police constables' wives were quite uneducated, unable to read or write, sew or knit. She started a knitting class, which became extremely popular, and would come home with piles of socks needing the heels turned and jumpers needing finishing; she wished she had been trained as an occupational therapist or a teacher.

Among the leisure activities we enjoyed in Arusha were riding — we were lent two horses and Geraldine took part in local races; trout fishing, as several rivers in the province were stocked with rainbow trout; and rough shooting (guinea fowl and partridge), in which our elder son participated at an early age.

Soon after I had taken over command of the police in Northern Province, we were to be the hosts of a number of visiting VIPs from outside Tanganyika. First, the Prince Aly Khan, the Aga Khan's heir-to-be, visited the province, where there was a sizeable community of Ismaili Khojas, the Aga Khan's followers. He was accompanied by none other than Rita Hayworth, who provided an additional inducement to attend receptions in his honour. It was amusing to note the number of colonial officials who were anxious to meet and converse with her — including myself.

Another visitor early in 1951 was the Governor-General of Madagascar, in whose honour we were directed by the Governor to ensure that the official banquet in his honour had local produce only. This gave the opportunity to those of us on station to spend a day fishing for rainbow trout on the Kikafu River on Mt Kilimanjaro, and we netted 147 trout with five rods, including taking 15 out of one pool.

* * *

The next four years exposed me to the full rigours and adrenaline of crisis management, first as provincial police commander and later as regional police commissioner. Early in 1951 the police were on full alert to enforce a particularly distasteful eviction of several thousand Meru tribesmen from their pastoral lands in the Sanya corridor between Mts Kilimanjaro and Meru (for details see Appendix E). This was followed by a spate of large-scale Masai cattle raids on the Wasukuma, the neighbouring tribe in the southern Serengeti area. For the first time we employed a spotter aircraft (piloted by a local settler/special constable) in operational cooperation with ground patrols.

By the end of 1952 it was obvious that we, in northern Tanganyika, could not remain detached from the Mau Mau rebellion in Kenya. There was a sizeable Kikuyu population (some 17,000) in the Northern Province of Tanganyika — a large force employed by the Forestry Department on the northern slopes of Kilimanjaro near Laitokitok and the remainder dispersed as labour on European-owned coffee estates in both the Moshi and Arusha districts. Prior to the outbreak of the rebellion and the declaration of a state of emergency in Kenya, the regional Special Branch officer in Moshi had received reports of illegal 'oathings', intimidation and assaults amongst the Kikuyu forest labour force and the existence of a Mau Mau cell on north Kilimanjaro. Coincidentally, I attended a regional police conference in Nyeri, Kenya in August 1952, at which the Kenya head of Special Branch played down the existence of a secret society amongst the Kikuyu, assuring us that it was a lawful movement, primarily bent on the restoration to the Kikuyu of alienated lands occupied by European settlers. This, notwithstanding a mass meeting held in Nyeri the previous weekend at which none other than Jomo Kenyatta had harangued the massed ranks of Kikuyu that these lands should be 'liberated'. We returned to northern Tanganyika determined not to be lulled into a false sense of security and prepared contingency plans to deal with any outbreak of lawlessness and violence among our Kikuyu population. I had under my command a company of motorized police (paramilitary) based at Moshi and they were promptly trained in field operations, as well as their more conventional role of riot control.

Soon after the outbreak of murders, cattle slashing, theft of firearms from European farms and widespread illegal 'oathing' within the Kikuyu population, we were faced with the external threat of infiltration by Mau Mau gangs over the Kenya/Tanganyika border. The first of these raids, bent on theft of firearms and intimidation of the resident Kikuyu population, was, on good field intelligence, ambushed in the West Meru Forest and the police unit, led by A. S. P. John Drury, inflicted heavy casualties on the gang and dispersed it. The leader of the gang broke ranks, shot a local Mwarusha dead and was finally run to earth and killed. His body was brought in a truck to my headquarters in Arusha. He proved to have been the leader of the gang.

Apart from brutal murders of 'loyal' (non-Mau Mau) Kikuyu in the province by Mau Mau activists, including one in which a whole family of six, including a pregnant woman and children, were slaughtered on the outskirts of Arusha, infiltration thereafter was confined to the Lolionda area of northern Masailand, which was mopped up by the motorized company after a 50-mile forced march through the Rift Valley in the Lake Natron area.

Apart from these two unwanted Mau Mau intrusions into Northern Province, there were virtually no other major incidents. However, this was largely due to the courageous decision by Sir Edward Twining, the governor, to accept the advice of his provincial commissioner, Bill Cadiz, and myself at a weekend meeting at the Governor's Lodge in Lushoto that the situation could only be contained if it were agreed to round up *all* Kikuyu in the province and detain them, in two designated detention areas, well away from the Kenya border, for the duration of the emergency in Kenya.

The identification and round-up involved deployment of all available forces for two weeks and then use of temporary holding areas (such as warehouses) in Arusha and Moshi until the detention areas at Tamota, near Handeni in Tanga Province and near Tabora in Western Province, were ready for occupation. The 17,000 Kikuyu men, women and children were reluctantly detained until the end of the Mau Mau emergency, then returned to their places of origin in Kenya.

During this period of my command in northern Tanganyika, forces available to the police service had faced confrontation between the administering authorities and the public; nevertheless, cooperation was eventually forthcoming from the African public, which recognized these crises as real threats to their lives and economic wellbeing and willingly came to the aid of the established authority.

* * *

Between 1954 and 1958 I was back in Dar es Salaam, having been promoted to the rank of deputy commissioner of police, and was now responsible for the administration and detailed inspection of the whole force. This took me to every single district headquarters and police station in the land and proved invaluable in understanding the very wide range of grass-roots problems in the country. Shortly after my assumption of duties as deputy commissioner, and in the absence of both the substantive commissioner (on UK leave) and the acting commissioner (*ad interim*) George Robins (at a conference in Nairobi), we were asked to provide police reinforcements to Nyasaland, which had declared a state of emergency because of widespread disturbances following Dr Hastings Banda's detention. This involved an airlift to Karonga in the Northern Province of the protectorate, which was promptly organized. However, most of the men had never been in an aircraft before and I was obliged to reassure them that there were toilet facilities on board before they were prepared to take off.

George Robins then left on the commissioner's return from leave to take up the post of commissioner of police in Cyprus where, before long, he was in the throes of the emergency there. Meanwhile, I had been selected to attend a course at the Joint Service Staff College in the UK and travelled to take advantage of this unexpected bonus, for my two sons were already at school in Britain. However, just as we had settled in to our rented cottage near Latimer, Bucks, the Colonial Office received a telegram from Dar es Salaam requesting me to return to my post because HRH The Princess Margaret was to pay a visit to Tanganyika and I would be required to organize and supervise all police and security arrangements during her visit, which was to last 11 days. I was obliged to acquiesce, though with ill-disguised reluctance.

* * *

During 1958 both the governor and the commissioner of police retired and I learned that I had been offered the post of commissioner of police (later inspector-general) in Uganda and was due to take over my new command early in 1959. In the interim, I acted as commissioner in Tanganyika for six months, pending the arrival of the new commissioner, Geoffrey Wilson, who had been transferred from Malaya and who officiated at the installation of the new governor, Sir Richard Turnbull, who was to be the last appointed before independence (in 1961).

* * *

Uhuru was in the air, elections were held and Julius Nyerere, as leader of TANU (Tanganyika National Union), led Tanganyika as it followed its inchoate progress to independence. Let it be said that, apart from mass meetings and the general air of expectancy and uncertainty, Tanganyika's final steps towards independence were encouragingly peaceful and there was little cause for police intervention except to control mass demonstrations.

At the same time, it was obvious that the process of 'local-ization' was belatedly slow, though, so far as the police force was concerned, we had already introduced accelerated promotion for potential Africans to district command post. It should be recorded that the provincial administration at the same time had only *one* African district commissioner in posts (Dunstan Omari) in 1959, a bare two years before independence. My own departure from Tanganyika for 'better things' in Uganda was a happy one with a string of farewell parties but, after 18 years' service in the country, with more than a tinge of regret.

7

Transition to Independence: A Retrospective Study of Uganda in Turmoil, 1959–64

O n arrival in Uganda from Tanganyika early in March 1959, to take up my appointment as commissioner of police, the first impression was of a prosperous, highly developed African society with excellent public services. The contrast with Tanganyika, in terms of conditions of service and material resources available to the police force, was marked, and, for a new incumbent of an important branch of the public service, most encouraging. Everything augured well for the progressive development of the force.

However, within ten days of arrival in the country, we were confronted with the first of the many emergencies that challenged the force in the next six years. With hindsight, it was the prelude to the chronicle of violence which has beset Churchill's 'Pearl of Africa' ever since.

In 1959, when we first went to Uganda, there were 120 gazetted police officers, all European; this soon changed as Africans were promoted and promotions increased rapidly as independence approached. We entertained many officers and their wives, but to begin with our social life was only among Europeans. When we first entertained African officers in our house it was difficult to persuade them to bring their wives, but when they eventually did so Geraldine found them better educated and more sophisticated than Tanganyikan African women. She made friends among them and became involved with their problems.

About 800 police constables with their families were housed at Nsambya Barracks, which were greatly in need of improvements. Geraldine frequently visited the clinic at the barracks where Mrs Blythe, wife of the police quartermaster, and Jessie Okondo, a Xhosa from South Africa, did their best to help and look after the hundreds of women under difficult conditions. Many of the women came from remote areas, had no education and only spoke their tribal languages, so often could not communicate with those from different tribes. Later, a welfare officer, Dorothy Isaac, and several African welfare assistants were appointed and conditions gradually improved.

An old friend of Geraldine's, Rosemary Byers, was the organizer of the Red Cross Blood Transfusion Service and Geraldine joined her in giving talks and showing a locally made film to try to overcome the great fear Africans had of giving blood. About twice a week they went out in their Peugeot van with a doctor and two African medical orderlies to take blood from volunteers at institutes, colleges, schools, the police and the prisons within a wide area round Kampala. (This was before the advent of AIDS.)

* * *

The Uganda National Movement (UNM), which was in essence a Baganda organization, declared a trade boycott directed primarily against the Asian retailer, whose presence was ubiquitous throughout the trading settlements in rural Buganda as well as in the major centres of population. The movement, with its slogan of 'Free-*dom*' accompanied by the V sign, enjoyed the active support of the many thousands of Baganda traders, farmers, middlemen and transporters, and the approval of most of the rest of the population in the kingdom. It had a strong local political impetus and rapidly developed xenophobic overtones. There was little doubt that it met with the tacit support of the Kabaka and his government in demonstrating Buganda 'muscle'. Although it never merited the imposition of a full state of emergency, it caused widespread dislocation of the country's economy, considerable damage to property and crops, and the deaths of a number of persons and injury to scores of others. In the first six months of the campaign there were no less than 610 incidents, including murders, bomb attacks (one on a mosque), arson, crop slashing, malicious damage to property and assaults on Asians. During the same six months 456 offenders were taken to court and 235 were convicted. The police force and, for that matter, the government machine were totally unprepared for prolonged violence of this nature, and it was necessary to introduce emergency measures to contain the situation.

Fortunately, there was standing legislation, embodied in the Police Ordinance of 1947, which could be applied on order of the governor in council. Upon declaration of a disturbed area, which was defined in geographical terms to cover the area of unrest, the commissioner of police was automatically empowered to impose conditions, which to many these days would appear to be draconian but which in prevailing circumstances were necessary and acted as an effective check to an uncontrolled spread of disorder.

These, *inter alia*, embraced the imposition of a curfew, a prohibition on carrying offensive weapons (spears, knives, knobkerries), the control and search of vehicles by the establishment of roadblocks, the impounding of privately owned firearms, the requisitioning of vehicles and the issue of restriction orders against known activists, amounting to house arrest. For the record, this legislation was retained and imposed when necessary by the government of Uganda after independence in 1962.

It is interesting to note that, because of the existence of this legislation, which was never challenged politically or in the courts, it was not necessary during the period under review (1959–64) for the government of Uganda to declare a state of emergency. There were no less than 27 occasions during those six turbulent years when, in the absence of such legislation, a state of emergency would have to have been declared. It made the enactment of a Public Order Ordinance largely irrelevant.

The outbreak of widespread violence also necessitated an urgent review of existing contingency plans and much closer and more regular liaison between the government and the security forces, both police and military. A central security committee was established, under the chairmanship of the governor, daily operations and crime situation reports were introduced, quarterly meetings of senior police officers were held, and regular weekly meetings with the chief secretary, as the minister responsible for law and order, were conducted to review current developments, to plan counter-measures and to identify priorities and security targets. These were in addition to the monthly local intelligence committee meetings, which had been in existence for some time past to assess security intelligence available to the protectorate government. In effect, these new measures activated the consciousness of the government in practical terms in monitoring the state of security of the protectorate, and paid off handsomely in the years to follow.

Despite the need to contain crime and civil disorder, the longer-term structural and training requirements of the police force were not overlooked. Although there had been a limited degree of 'localization' of some of the junior command posts in the force by the promotion to gazetted (commissioned) rank of outstanding African officers, there were still some 250 British and Asian expatriate officers in the force. Such 'localization' as had taken place had been on an *ad hoc* basis and it was decided, with the inevitability of independence sooner rather than later, to review the potential of Ugandan African officers serving in the force to assume greater responsibility and exercise genuine command functions.

Sir Andrew Cohen, a former governor of Uganda, had once said that the only effective training in responsibility was the genuine exercise of responsibility, so it was agreed to pursue this admirable and realistic objective. The initiative came from the force itself rather than from the protectorate government. The then chief secretary was of the opinion that independence was many years ahead; my own recent experience as deputy commissioner and latterly acting commissioner of police in Tanganyika led me to think otherwise, and a progressive phased internal plan was introduced for the 'localization' of junior and intermediate command posts, particularly in the operational areas. In this we were given invaluable assistance by the United Kingdom police authorities and a special command course was organized by the West York-shire Constabulary at Wakefield, to which selected Ugandan officers were sent for management training. This followed the pattern of training given to the Nigerian police, who had already benefited from a similar series of courses at Wakefield. In effect, this programme resulted in over 100 executive command posts at all levels being filled by Ugandan officers by independence at the end of 1962. Thus, it might be said that the force could be seen to be predominantly commanded by Ugandans on Independence Day on 9 October 1962.

* * *

By April 1959 the force was extended on operations not only in Buganda, where the boycott campaign continued unabated, but also on the Sudan border where the remnants of the 1955 army mutiny in the southern Sudan, who had been active in the Tereteinia mountains since Sudan's independence, extended their hit-and-run attacks into the Kitgum District of northern Uganda. This group of ex-mutineers was led by a former Sudanese army NCO called Latada, who had acquired for himself a Robin Hood reputation among the Nilotic inhabitants of Torit District of the Sudan.

Ambushes and individual armed attacks on Sudanese army personnel and on the administration had been successfully carried out for several years, and the Sudanese authorities were obliged to accept the fact that much of the area was no longer under effective administrative or police control. The problem was tackled by punitive raids of considerable savagery by the army garrison based on Juba, the headquarters of Equatoria Province Command. These were conducted from main lines of communication and, apart from loss of life amongst the civilian population, had little real impact on the rebel groups operating from mountainous and inaccessible bases. It could be said that the Latada revolt was the genesis of the much larger 'Anyanya' rebellion by the southern Sudanese some ten years later.

So far as the security forces in Uganda were concerned, the extension of Latada's activities into Ugandan territory posed a problem of new and very different dimensions from previous out-breaks of civil disorder. It required a capability to deploy and operate mobile field units in wild, difficult and largely uninhabited terrain. In the absence of adequate paramilitary resources, it was necessary to enlist the assistance of the army (King's African Rifles), marking the first of many police/military combined operations which were to take place in the next few years. Combined police/military units were dispatched to the Kitgum District and a series of sweeps were mounted in areas in which the Sudanese rebels were known to be active, with some success. A number of engagements resulted from the operations and some members of the gangs were killed, wounded or captured by either the Sudanese or Uganda forces, but neither Latada nor any of his principal lieutenants was captured. Latada and two of the leading gang leaders were to die of wounds or sickness in the bush some three years later.

✳ ✳ ✳

The UNM boycott continued and the full provisions of the Police Ordinance were brought into force by the declaration of the whole of Buganda as a 'disturbed area'. Peri-urban sweeps were continued in the Kibuga area of Kampala, and large numbers of boycott ringleaders were arrested and placed under restriction orders. The most prominent were 'deported' to a specially constructed camp in Karamoja. Here again standing legislation of considerable vintage was used (Deportation Ordinance, which in effect meant 'rustication' within the protectorate).

May 1959 was also marked by a very serious riot in the government prison at Lira in Lango District, in which a senior British police officer was severely injured and had subsequently to leave the service prematurely on medical grounds; and by a visit by a party from the United States' War College, who were briefed on the current security situation in Uganda. Internal development measures in the force were pursued, despite the security commitments in the country, and a force welfare department was established as well as a police association to represent all ranks of the force. These measures were directed at much greater representation and participation of selected members of the force at all levels in welfare and general conditions of service.

Having commanded the Uganda Police Force for just over four eventful months, we were paid an inspection visit by the inspector-general of colonial police, Sir Ivo Stourton, who himself had been a former commissioner of police in Uganda. This was particularly welcome, as it came at a time when many changes were in train and the support of the Colonial Office was vital. This was readily forthcoming, particularly in the organization of command training for Ugandan officers in the United Kingdom.

* * *

A fresh operational area of Lake Victoria added a further burden on police resources. At the end of June a combined air and amphibious operation was carried out by the police sections on smugglers, illegal arms manufacturers and other criminal elements in the area of southeast Busoga District's offshore islands. Several gangs were surprised while poaching fish and operating illicit liquor stills, and from this date onwards periodic sweeps were mounted in this area.

A party from the Imperial Defence College in Britain visited Uganda during the month, and again it was my duty to brief the visitors on the current security situation in Uganda. The month also saw the introduction of a plan to establish a women's section in the Uganda police. As previously in Tanganyika, a British woman police inspector was seconded from the United Kingdom to organize, train and supervise the unit. We were fortunate to obtain the services, in both instances, of outstanding officers, and the fact that there are still active professional women police officers in both countries over 20 years later is ample testimony to their efforts.

* * *

At the beginning of November 1960, the first effects of increasing intertribal tension and conflict in neighbouring Rwanda between the majority Hutu and the minority Tutsi tribesmen became evident with the steady flow of Tutsi, Batwa and Tutsi-sympathetic refugees across the international border into Uganda.

It was necessary for the government of Uganda, in the circumstances, to establish refugee camps close to the Rwanda border in Ankole District. International aid agencies were swift to provide clothing and food in support, though little foresight was exercised, with the result that many hundreds of tons of American yellow maize flour found their way into the local Asian black market rather than into the mouths of the refugees, who found the diet both alien and unpalatable. The siting of the refugee holding areas in the proximity of the Rwanda border proved to be another error, as it enabled militant Tutsi activists to mount armed raids into their former homeland. The tragic and bloody sequel to this misjudgement was to take place some four years later (see below).

The year ended with a visit by the secretary of state for the colonies to Uganda on a familiarization tour. A meeting was held at Government House, which I attended, to outline the internal security situation in the protectorate.

✳ ✳ ✳

The new year, 1960, was heralded by a visit to Uganda by the secretary general of the United Nations, Mr Dag Hammarskjöld. Again, I was involved in a briefing session at Government House, Entebbe.

In the third week of January, some of the most serious and widespread riots ever experienced in Uganda broke out in Bukedi District in the Eastern Province. The background to the riots, which were primarily directed against the local authorities, was a mounting wave of dissatisfaction against the graduated tax assessments made by the chiefs. There is little doubt that these were often both arbitrary and inequable, and hit the poorer elements of the population. At the same time, political forces, particularly those of the district's minority Roman Catholic Democratic Party, exploited the people's general unease and dissatisfaction. Politico-religious polarization in the community was becoming evident in a country already beset by tribal and factional strains.

The provincial administration underestimated the lack of confidence in the chiefs and, despite frequent and vociferous opposition voiced at *barazas* to the introduction of the new graduated tax, was of the opinion that the unrest was being stimulated by a disgruntled minority. However, when the riots broke out, they were of a general nature and directed at all local authority presence. Every *saza* (county) and *gombolola* (parish) headquarters was attacked, as were all local authority police stations and barracks.

Protectorate police security forces were drafted into the area in strength, but it was evident after the first 24 hours' rioting that they could not contain the situation. A 'disturbed area' was declared and a battalion of the Uganda Rifles (4th KAR) joined the police forces in the area, acting in aid of the civil power. After several days' operations, during which 12 persons were killed, several hundred injured and over 1200 arrests made, order was restored. Thousands of pounds of damage was done to local authority property throughout the district, chiefly by arson.

A commission of inquiry, under the chairmanship of a West African judge, was appointed and the whole system of graduated tax was revised; many chiefs were relieved of their duties and a network of central government police posts was established throughout the district. The commission of inquiry commended both the central government police and the Uganda Rifles for their restrained conduct during the operations.

* * *

Towards the end of January, a second wave of refugees from intertribal disturbances began to cross the Ankole/Kigezi borders into Uganda. Again they were predominantly from the Tutsi minority who had for so long enjoyed overlordship of the country. Although the Hutu reactions could be largely ascribed to tribalism, there was undoubtedly an element of a 'peasant revolt' in the outbreak of violence.

The Uganda protectorate government drew up plans not only for refugee relief but also for resettlement in Uganda for the many hundreds who had little or no hope of returning to their homes in Rwanda. For the Tutsi, who were predominantly pastoralists, the adjustment to an agricultural life was difficult. However, when three resettlement areas in western Buganda and in the Toro kingdom, well away from the border, were established, the Tutsi rapidly changed their lifestyle and adapted to the agricultural environment. The fact that there was a tribal affinity between the Baganda and Batoro and their Tutsi/Bahima cousins assisted in the process.

It was during this month that British troops visited Uganda for the first time since the First World War. On a short holiday visit to Kenya I arranged, with the agreement of the protectorate government, for a party of 2nd battalion Coldstream Guards, then stationed in Kenya, to pay a courtesy visit to Uganda. The corps of drums accompanied the party and beat the retreat in both Entebbe and Kampala. The Kabaka of Buganda, himself an honorary captain in the Grenadier Guards, donned his ceremonial uniform and took the salute in Kampala. This was an excellent injection of public relations, as tension between the protectorate government and the Kabaka was high at the time.

* * *

During the month of June, intensification of rifle-armed Turkana cattle raids into northeast Karamoja District necessitated the deployment of several units of the Uganda Police Special Force (paramilitary units) to the area. These units, drawn from the main force, consisted of approximately 40 men, divided into three sections, each with its section commander, driver and signaller, plus a small command section. They were formed early in the year to meet the increasing threat to civil order both in the towns and in the field. They were entirely self-supporting, with their own transport, riot control equipment, arms and ammunition, signal equipment and rations, and could operate in the field for up to 72 hours without relief. As the personnel were without exception regular trained police officers, secondment to the units was on a two-year rotational basis. They were to prove themselves time and again over the period 1959–64. They provided a well-trained, versatile, first-line strike force, thus avoiding the need to call on military support other than in a major emergency. (They were disbanded in July 1971 by Idi Amin, who misguidedly saw them as a threat to his own ill-disciplined rabble of an army.)

During the June raids by the Turkana, who were armed with old Austrian Steyr rifles, smuggled in from Ethiopia or bartered for camels, there were a number of clashes with the Uganda Police Special Force. In one of these, 12 fatalities were inflicted by the police on the raiders. On 22 June a young British assistant superintendent of police, Tony Weedon, on his first tour, was shot and killed in a running engagement with Turkana raiders in the Oropoi valley area of the Uganda–Kenya border. His body was flown back from this remote corner of Uganda and he was buried with full service honours in Kampala.

Deterioration in the situation towards the end of the month, when the police special units were overstretched, called for military reinforcements. RAF Beverley transport aircraft (based in Nairobi) were used for the first time in moving troops and additional police into the operational area. The raids were checked and an uneasy peace restored between the Karamojong and the Turkana.

* * *

Towards the end of the month, I paid a flying visit to the Congo border area, visiting Belgian administrative headquarters at Mahagi in Orientale Province and Rutshuru in Kivu, in anticipation of Congo independence, which was due on the 30th of the month. From what I heard and saw, it was obvious that the Belgian administration was going to bale out and leave the Congolese to their own devices — and chaos. Practically nothing had been done to prepare the Congolese for the responsibilities of self-government — the most senior African at regional headquarters in Mahagi was a filing clerk. The catch phrase among the Belgians was, '*Nous quittons le camp.*' This boded ill for the future and I returned to Entebbe to ask for authority to reinforce all Uganda police border posts and to have armed mobile reserves on stand-by for 30 June.

On 9 July 1960 the Congo crisis broke and the influx of European refugees commenced. During the next ten days between 4500 and 5000 Belgian and other European refugees, men, women and children, sought sanctuary in Uganda from the Congo. The first to come were the officials (administration, police, agricultural and veterinary officers) and their families; next the planters, whose relative isolation made them soft targets for marauding bands of mutinous soldiers of the so-called Armée nationale congolaise; and finally the businessmen and traders. Most of the missionaries, often misguidedly as it proved, remained on their stations — and relied, in the words of an American who refused later to be evacuated by a rescue mission mounted from Uganda, on the 'protection of the Almighty'. There was a similar flight of Europeans from the Congo into Tanganyika, though on a smaller scale. All refugees arriving at Uganda police border posts were documented and those who had firearms, of whom there were many, were disarmed. Most of them were destitute and without adequate means for subsistence for more than a few days.

The Uganda government immediately set up an emergency refugee organization, under the administration of a senior official, Mr (now Sir) Richard Posnett, later governor of Bermuda; public transport was commandeered to transport those who arrived on foot at the border to Kampala; and reception centres were set up. Large numbers of local volunteers, many of them wives of European officials and businessmen in Kampala and Entebbe, manned the centres and first aid clinics, and gave invaluable and tireless assistance to the authorities around the clock. The Uganda Red Cross and St John Ambulance organizations were mobilized to assist in the mammoth task of dealing with the influx, which included considerable numbers of children and babies. Such was the confusion in the early stages that children were separated from their parents *en route* and had to be reunited after arrival in Kampala. We even found two 6-month-old Belgian babies lying unclaimed in an empty bus in one of the reception centres.

Refugees arrived in Kampala at all hours of the day and night, crammed into cars and buses. With many other women, Geraldine helped unload and assist them and helped man the canteen, open 24 hours a day, with food and drink. Police assistance was given in providing temporary accommodation in transit, and rescue operations were directed from a special operations room established in a flat in the police officers' mess. This was to be used later as a clandestine control room, linked by radio with American

48

mission stations in the Congo's Orientale Province, through which a number of airborne rescue operations were mounted with the assistance of volunteer light aircraft pilots from Kenya. Many scores of American mission personnel and their families were literally plucked from remote airstrips many hundreds of miles inside the Congo by these brave men and women.

After the successful evacuation of most of the Europeans from the Congo, several of these pilots were decorated by the Belgian government. Harrowing tales of harassment by the Congolese army were brought out by many of the refugees, including robbery, rape and, in a few cases, brutal killing. One small convoy of refugees was ambushed by pygmies in the Ituri Forest and their vehicles seized. They were left to continue their journey to the Uganda border and safety on foot. We learned later that some of the pygmies converted the stolen cars into dwelling places and, in one case, omitting to drain the petrol tank, lit a fire in the car and were blown up — poetic justice?

It took some months to settle the affairs of the refugees and arrange their homeward transport through Kenya to Europe. Local residents were asked to take in families, and we had one family (a teacher, his wife and three children) with us in our home for several weeks. In the wake of the European refugees came many Afro-Europeans, sympathetic Africans and, again later, deserters from the Congolese army. The latter were disarmed and encouraged to return to the Congo when the heat was off and absorb themselves in their communities.

* * *

The election campaign for the *Lukiiko* (Buganda Parliament) was marked by inter-party intimidation. This followed the usual pattern of disorder in Buganda with crop-slashing, arson and assaults. Police reinforcements, both uniformed and CID, were drafted to the rural areas of the kingdom where most of the intimidation was taking place.

The governor, Sir Frederick Crawford, took the opportunity both of a visit to Uganda by Iain Macleod, the Secretary of State for the Colonies, to open the new parliamentary buildings, and a private visit by Earl Mountbatten, for a briefing on the current situation in the country. During my prepared outline of the problems that beset Uganda, I was somewhat surprised to be told by Mountbatten that the situation was similar to the one he had faced in Hyderabad.

* * *

During the same month, under the auspices of the USIS, Louis Armstrong and party visited Uganda and gave an open-air concert at Nakivubo stadium in the centre of Kampala, which was attended by a rapturous crowd of over 3000 persons. As a jazz 'buff' I was equally rapturous and met the great man at a reception given by the American consul-general afterwards. When I reminded him that I had first attended one of his prewar concerts at the Holborn Empire in London, he countered with the remark, 'We're old, man!'

At the end of the month the annual PAFMECA (Pan-African Freedom Movement in East and central Africa) conference was held for the first time on Ugandan soil at Mbale in the Eastern Province.

Early in the month no. 8 flight of the army reconnaissance squadron of the Army Air Corps from Kenya carried out feasibility trials on all border airstrips in Uganda. During operations, one Auster aircraft was written off after an emergency landing in bad weather near Kabale in southwest Uganda. There were no casualties.

* * *

In the same month, the dispute between the Buganda and Banyoro kingdoms over the 'lost counties' of Buyaga and Bugangadzi in west Buganda came to a head. There was large-scale intimidation and violence between the Baganda and Banyoro, and the Banyoro living in the two countries revolted against 'alien' Baganda local authorities. Uganda Police Special Force (paramilitary) reinforcements were drafted in and a number of temporary police posts established to control the situation. This was the first major manifestation of a serious challenge to Buganda's claim to the 'lost countries'. Strife between the two tribal factions was to continue for the next eight years and become a permanent peace keeping burden on the Uganda police.

* * *

Ever since the first constitutional conference in London in August/ September 1960, the Buganda government, with the active encouragement of the Kabaka, Freddie Mutesa, became more and more intransigent in its attitude to pooling its resources with the rest of Uganda, and a campaign for secession from the protectorate was mounted. The declared 'plan' was to secede from the rest of Uganda on 1 January 1961, and preparations were made throughout the kingdom to give effect to this intention. Thus, the protectorate government was faced with the likelihood of open rebellion in Buganda at the end of the month.

It was therefore decided to move 2000 extra police into Buganda by the middle of the month, and I arranged for an armed police flag march of over 800 officers and men through the centre of Kampala on 12 December. Flanked by the mayor of Kampala (Kulubya — a traditionalist Muganda himself) and the British resident commissioner (Dick Stone), I took the salute as column after column of armed police marched past.

A reserve battalion of the King's African Rifles was moved from Nakuru in Kenya to Jinja to reinforce the Uganda military forces, and security was tightened up at all main centres in Buganda and, in particular, in Kampala and Entebbe. In the event, such was the preparedness of the security forces that the Baganda, whose plan for secession in any case had not been rationalized, were unable on the night of 31 December/1 January to do anything positive, consoling themselves with ineffectual threats of violence and a great deal of brave talk. This was the measure of determination of the Buganda secessionists in the face of a superior and determined counterforce. I personally was accused publicly by two Baganda ministers of 'sabre-rattling', but such was the nature of the situation that, had the protectorate government not taken a firm and forceful stance, the Baganda would have exploited it and there

51

would have been a chain reaction throughout the country. The movement for secession was stillborn and it was not long before the population in Buganda as a whole forgot the brave promises of the last quarter of 1960.

* * *

The so-called Relationships Commission, led by Lord Munster, visited Uganda in 1961 to examine the relationships of the component parts of the country and, in particular, that of the kingdoms in preparing for constitutional advance prior to independence. The determination of the British government to guide Uganda to independence without sweeping aside traditional and tribal loyalties and institutions was undoubtedly with the best of intentions, but in my opinion, in the longer term, was a disservice to the emerging nation. The fact that Buganda's bluff was called should surely have been an indication that the creation of a unitary state *before* independence was by no means impossible.

The pattern of constitutional safeguards and counterbalances enshrined in the independence constitution was to be rapidly dismantled first by Obote and later by Amin.

* * *

As a result of the continuing chaos and lawlessness in those parts of the Congo adjoining Uganda, and to safeguard against incursions into Uganda by undisciplined and aggressive Congolese government troops, in February 1961 both Special Force (police) and Uganda Rifles units were moved up to the border. In addition, a company of the Tanganyika Rifles (2nd/6th KAR) was deployed in support on the Ankole/Bukoba border.

Also, the US Assistant Secretary of State for African Affairs, G. Mennen ('Soapy') Williams, visited Uganda during an African 'fact-finding' tour and made a number of naïve and offensive statements about 'the evils of residual colonialism', which had little or no impact on local African nationalists. The fact that he was entertained by the resident American CIA officer made his self-appointed role of redeemer even less plausible. I met him at a reception and found his preconceived ideas of decolonization childish, facile and slightly ridiculous. The American consulate-general staff found him embarrassing.

* * *

The first parliamentary elections to be held in Uganda took place in March in an atmosphere of tension. There was widespread intimidation in Buganda where resistance was hardening in traditionalist and conservative rural areas against any form of representative government that was not essentially Baganda in nature. From Mengo (in the heart of Buganda and the site of the Kabaka's palace), a concerted campaign was mounted through county and parish chiefs to undermine the electoral process, and a partial boycott resulted. As a result of Buganda non-cooperation in the election, the leader of the Democratic Party, which was largely Catholic, Benedicto Kiwanuka, a prominent Muganda lawyer, assumed office as the first chief minister of Uganda. (He was to be murdered later during the Amin regime.)

* * *

At the end of the month, a large contingent of Malaysian troops passed through Uganda to join the UN peacekeeping force in the eastern Congo. A contingent from the Republic of Ireland had already been established in Kivu Province, and had cooperated with the Uganda police in preserving peace on the Uganda/Congo border. We had provided them with radio equipment to communicate with the Uganda police network and were in daily contact. I paid a number of liaison visits to their forward units in the Rutshuru area of Kivu Province, and we entertained officers and NCOs on their occasional visits to Kampala.

The Malaysian units, comprising a federal battalion and supporting services, were multiracial consisting of Malays, Chinese and Indians, under the command of senior British officers. Cross-border liaison was speedily and effectively re-established. The standard of discipline and turnout was very high and, of all the UN contingents posted to the eastern Congo, the Malaysians were without doubt the most effective and respected. In contrast, the UN contingent in Orientale Province, to the northwest of Uganda, was composed of Ethiopians. Although their officers were professionals and conducted themselves with restraint, the rank and file were reported to indulge in looting and rape. Congolese citizens who fled to Uganda stated categorically that the Ethiopians were no better than the rabble of the Armée nationale congolaise. Over the next two years, we were to have a succession of UN contingents (including Nigerian and Indonesian) in the eastern Congo, but, with the departure of the Malaysians, the close cooperation, first established with the Irish, died. The subsequent limbo paved the way for the disintegration of the peacekeeping process and the civil war which raged during the Mulelist era (1963–4).

* * *

A Sudanese government and police delegation visited Uganda to discuss closer coordination of security measures in the troubled border area between the southern Sudan and Uganda.

* * *

A renewal of large-scale armed raids by Turkana tribesmen into northeast Karamoja led to further combined military/police operations in the border area. A number of additional police posts were established and garrisoned. Heavy casualties were inflicted on the Turkana.

During these raids, the first batch of Teachers East Africa, mostly from the United States, arrived at Makerere University College. I spoke to them about the current security situation in Uganda and advised them on basic self-protection procedures. Most were completely unfamiliar with life in Africa and had an oversimplified concept of their role as educational 'liberators' from colonialism. Also, Mrs Indira Gandhi visited Uganda on a fact-finding mission. She was welcomed in all quarters, both officially and privately, and showed a realistic appreciation of the dilemma of the Indian community in the country. I met her at a reception at the Kabaka's palace (the Twekobe) on Mengo Hill and had a brief informal discussion with her later at a dinner given by the chief minister, Kiwanuka.

* * *

In September, renewed intertribal (Hutu/Tutsi) fighting in Rwanda led to a mass influx of Tutsi and their supporters into southwest Uganda. The collective total of Rwanda refugees was now reaching the 40,000 mark and new resettlement areas had to be established, administered and policed. Security measures were tightened to check the insidious development in the resettlement areas of a militant group known as the Inyenzi (cockroaches) who were planning reprisal raids into Rwanda against the new Belgian-supported Hutu regime. Reports were also received of arms smuggling from the Congo in support of the Inyenzi. Arms discovered in the refugee camps included American-made Thompson sub-machine-guns. The Mwami (King) of Rwanda sought political asylum in Uganda where he was a welcome guest of the Kabaka and an embarrassment to the protectorate government.

* * *

As the date for internal self-government in Uganda drew nearer and the prospect of exclusive autonomy of the kingdoms became dimmer, so the anti-Democratic Party campaign in Buganda increased. Attacks on Democratic Party supporters in rural areas increased and a number of political murders were committed. Minor riots took place in a number of centres in rural Buganda. Most of Buganda remained subject to disturbed area restrictions during the last quarter of 1961.

* * *

Sir Walter Coutts assumed the office of governor of Uganda, after many years of administrative service in Kenya and a short stint as administrator of St Lucia in the West Indies. The flow of refugees from Rwanda continued unabated and was now becoming a major burden on the resources of Uganda. HRH The Duke of Edinburgh visited Uganda *en route* to and from the Tanganyika independence celebrations. Together with senior administration and police officers, I was in attendance at Entebbe airport.

* * *

A commission of inquiry of privy councillors, led by Lord Listowel, visited Uganda in connection with the Buganda/Bunyoro 'lost counties' dispute. Evidence of the incidence of violence and intimidation was submitted to the commission, and discreet protective security was provided for the group throughout the visit.

* * *

Another large-scale military/police operation had to be mounted in northeast Karamoja against a renewal of armed raids by Turkana. This problem had by now assumed chronic dimensions and involved the permanent deployment of over 500 police on field and containment operations in the district.

* * *

Lukiiko (Buganda Parliament) elections to form an electoral college took place during the month, as a prelude to the May 1962 general election. They resulted in an overwhelming victory for the newly formed Kabaka Yekka (Kabaka Alone) Party, which had its roots in the traditionalist Baganda rural areas. The Democratic Party was largely eliminated in Buganda.

The month was marked by increased tension on two fronts; on the Rwanda border where retaliatory raids were mounted by militant Tutsi into Rwanda, and in the 'lost counties' on the Buganda/Bunyoro border where there was intertribal fighting. Police Special Force reinforcements were drafted into both areas.

* * *

The centenary of Speke's discovery of the source of the Nile was marked by celebrations and a tattoo at Jinja, on Lake Victoria, on 28 July. The discovery of the Ripon Falls, now dwarfed by the huge Owen Falls Dam and hydroelectric station, was re-enacted on the public recreation ground overlooking the lake, in the presence of the Kyabazinga of Busoga, William Wilberforce Nadiope (later to be the first minister of internal affairs and to be knighted by Her Majesty the Queen). He brought twentieth-century 'magic' with him and was seen busily recording the event with his Polaroid camera. Coincidentally, we had a descendant of Sir Samuel Baker-Peter (now Dr) Baker — staying with us, who joined in the celebrations.

During the month the Republic of Rwanda and the Kingdom of Burundi were granted independence by Belgium.

* * *

On 31 August the first outbreak of tribal disturbances between the Bakonjo and Baamba tribes and the government of the Kingdom of Toro in western Uganda took place on the southeastern slopes of the Ruwenzori mountains. The Bakonjo/Baamba group of tribes inhabited the foothills of the Ruwenzori and were ethnically separate from the Batoro. In many ways, there was a parallel here with the tribal divisions of Rwanda (for example, a predominantly Hima hierarchy and a Bantu proletariat). Most local government posts, including those in the Bakonjo/ Baamba areas, were held by Batoro, and tax and other revenues were paid into the Toro government treasury. Bakonjo/Baamba tribesmen attacked and burned Toro government offices and assaulted individual Batoro living in the affected areas. These disturbances rapidly developed into a major revolt which persisted for several years. Here again, extra police had to be deployed into the disturbed areas and existing central government police stations and posts were reinforced.

* * *

In the same month, I led a Uganda government delegation on a liaison visit to Juba, the capital of Equatoria Province of the Sudan, to discuss with the Sudanese army and police closer coordination of border security measures against anti-Sudanese rebel groups. Thus, in the month before Ugandan independence the security forces were deployed in strength in two widely separated disturbed areas.

* * *

The constitutional and administrative preparations for Ugandan independence had been proceeding apace during the first nine months of 1962, and a *modus vivendi* had hopefully been reached between an elected central government and the kingdoms and semi-autonomous Busoga. Milton Obote, leader of the Uganda People's Congress, in a coalition with the traditionalist Buganda Kabaka Yekka Party, had comfortably defeated the Democratic Party, and the protectorate was to be handed over to an elected African government on 9 October 1962. Serious doubts were entertained as to the credibility of the Uganda People's Congress/ Kabaka Yekka alliance, as support depended on two disparate power bases. However, it was no time for doubts, and constitutional safeguards were considered, wishfully or otherwise, sufficient to ensure a workable government.

So far as the Uganda police service was concerned, it was essential to settle on a plan for localization of all command posts so that the newly independent Uganda could be seen to be policed by Ugandans. As stated earlier, a phased and progressive plan had been laid as early as 1960 for all executive posts in the districts to be localized by Independence Day. This had gone well and the target of over one hundred posts to be filled by Ugandan officers who had undergone command training in the United Kingdom was met.

There was still the question of senior command, specialist and technical posts to be resolved. While on leave in the United Kingdom during the early summer of 1962, I had arranged to meet the Chief Minister (Obote) and the Minister of Internal Affairs (Nadiope) at St Ermin's Hotel in London, for a discussion on how best we could plan the future of the police service in an independent Uganda. It was agreed that, in order to give Ugandan African officers practical experience of command and executive responsibility, I should remain as inspector-general of police for up to two years after independence, and that key professional, specialist and technical posts should for the time being continue to be occupied by expatriate officers. Those expatriates whose posts could be filled by trained African officers should be 'induced' to retire prematurely with compensation for loss of career, and those whose services were to be retained should similarly be 'induced' to remain. This was done by improved contracts of service and bonus pension rights for each year of additional service. I made it clear to Obote that, although I was willing to remain in post after independence, to assist as best I could to ensure an orderly and peaceful transition of power, I doubted whether he could politically sustain the retention of an expatriate chief of police for more than two years after Independence Day, and informed him that I would give six months' notice of intention to retire in April 1964. To this he readily agreed, but there was an interesting sequel to this agreement, of which more anon.

Having laid the pattern of transfer of responsibility, my main preoccupation, on returning to Uganda from leave in mid-June, was to prepare for the independence celebrations. My deputy, Bob Langley, had done much of the groundwork in my absence, but shortly after my return it was decided to establish an independence celebration committee with Dick Posnett, permanent secretary from Entebbe, in charge. I suggested that it would help with the practical arrangements for the event if I were to second two very senior police officers to his committee. This was agreed and, without taking too much of the credit for the police, the smooth and highly successful programme was in no small degree due to the wise and intelligent advice and planning of these two officers (Jim Watson and Denys Drayton).

An interesting sidelight to the independence programme was the decision to organize it without the assistance of the ubiquitous Colonel Hefford, the independence 'expert'. Prior to my departure on leave, with the agreement of the governor and the chief minister, I had visited Tanganyika to consult with the authorities on their independence celebrations, which took place at the end of 1961. I received the maximum of cooperation and, as a result, probably saved the Ugandan taxpayer many thousands of pounds.

We did not pay Colonel Hefford a commission for borrowed ideas.

Despite security preoccupations in both the Ruwenzori and the Sudan border, a fully comprehensive police operations plan was drawn up to cover country-wide ceremonial parades, protective security for senior politicians and visiting VIPs, and traffic, parking and crowd control measures. The director of music of the Uganda police band composed the Ugandan national anthem, and the government was persuaded to strike an independence medal to be awarded to outstanding citizens, both high and low, and to the public services.

In all these complex arrangements we, in the police, were given maximum support by the Uganda Rifles. The regiment was fortunate, at this crucial time in the history of Uganda, to be commanded by an outstanding British officer — Bill Cheyne. Apart from requiring high standards from the army, he was also well liked by the politicians and the public at large. Sadly, in the ranks of the senior Ugandan officers was a recently promoted *effendi* — Idi Amin.

To digress briefly, Amin, who was nothing better, in military terms, than a sergeant-major, was among the handful of Ugandan NCOs who had been selected in 1959 as *effendis* (the equivalent of VCOs in the Indian Army). In his case it was widely believed that this was because he played rugby football, had boxed for Uganda and was generally considered by the seconded British officers as a 'good chap'. In 1961, during one of the operations against the Turkana, he had, as a platoon commander, been guilty of murder. Two captured Turkana had been tied to posts and left in the sun all day. They were dead by nightfall. The offence took place in the border area of Karamoja/Turkana — on Kenyan soil. A police investigation was opened and, after completion of inquiries, a prima-facie case of murder was revealed.

However, with independence pending in Uganda and later in Kenya, it was decided by the two governors, on the advice of the attorneys-general, not to press the charge but to hand him over for 'military discipline'. Some years later, Sir Walter Coutts, the governor of Uganda, confirmed this in a letter to *The Times*. Had the law taken its course, it is reasonable to assume that history would have been changed and many thousands of Ugandan lives spared. However, Idi Amin survived and, as a captain, played a prominent part in the independence ceremonial.

HRH the Duke of Kent, accompanied by the Duchess, represented Her Majesty the Queen at the independence celebrations; Milton Obote became the first prime minister of an independent Uganda; Sir Walter Coutts remained as governor-general; and the programme went off without a hitch.

* * *

After independence, social life became very different; gone were the formal gatherings of government officials and, with the coming of numerous foreign embassies, there was much more variety. African women took to official parties with delight, changing from bare feet to high-heeled shoes and nylons, even wearing hats and gloves, which were still the fashion on some formal occasions.

During the summer holidays, when our sons were with us, we enjoyed visiting the remote areas of Karamoja, travelling mostly by Land-Rover driven by Abok, my police driver for six years. Roads in some areas were almost non-existent, just rocky mountain tracks or game paths through high 'buffalo' grass where we could be delayed by elephants reluctant to move out of the way. Chris Treen, the senior pilot of the Police Air Wing flew us all over Uganda in the police Cessna. He was prepared to land wherever there was a small open space or open road — and often did so. In their vacations our sons managed to get temporary employment. Brian taught at a boys' secondary school one year, and found that he was younger than anyone in his class. And during another summer vacation he managed a refugee camp on the Rwanda border. Both he and Tony were involved respectively in independence and first anniversary celebrations in Uganda. Tony wrote his Oxford finals thesis on Kampala.

Shortly after independence Prime Minister Milton Obote was married to Miria, a Muganda woman, at Namirembe Cathedral. The service was taken by Archbishop Brown, the first archbishop of Uganda. The cathedral was packed and several thousand people attended the reception which was held at the Lugogo Sports

Stadium. It is the only wedding we have been to at which we were each handed a bottle of champagne (and a glass) on arrival.

✳ ✳ ✳

The conclusion of the independence celebrations saw an intensification of the Bakonjo/Baamba revolt in the Ruwenzori. A local leader, Mukirane, had emerged and, when under pressure from the security forces, conducted his campaign from across the border in the Congo. Disturbances were widespread throughout the Ruwenzori region, particularly in Bakonjo South. Toro local government chiefs, teachers and even nursing personnel were driven out of the county and there was much arson and damage to property.

In the circumstances, believing that the impasse could only be solved politically, Obote decided to 'commission' Tom Stacey, of the *Evening Standard*, to carry out a special assignment. Stacey, who was a prominent journalist in the United Kingdom and who had previous knowledge of the area, was to seek out and contact Mukirane, the leader of the rebels, with a view to calling off the revolt and coming to terms with the newly independent Uganda government. With both Ugandan police and military assistance, Stacey was able to penetrate the Bakonjo 'lines', and contacted Mukirane. He obtained much valuable information but was unsuccessful in his mission. Police and military operations continued against the rebels.[1]

---

1. I learned in November 1981, over 19 years after the first outbreak of violence, that the Ruwenzori revolt continued and that Mukirane elevated himself to the status of 'king' and actively directed the rebels. The government of Uganda subsequently mounted a military operation to hunt down Mukirane. Seven truckloads of troops arrived at Kagondo in the southern foothills of the Ruwenzori and set forth on foot to search for him. They returned empty-handed, as he had obviously, as in the past, slipped over the border into Zaire (Congo). However, as on so many operations carried out by the Ugandan army, they left their mark. For days afterwards local villagers were seeking medical treatment at the mission hospital for severed fingers, ears and other wanton wounds inflicted upon them by the soldiers.

* * *

On a happier note, the Ugandan Commonwealth Games team left for Perth, Western Australia, in October. As president of the Ugandan Olympic and Commonwealth Games Association, president of the Ugandan AAA, and vice-president of the Uganda ABA, I took a close personal interest in their fortunes, more especially as, over the previous six months, we had managed to raise half the funds for the tour by public subscription and appeals. The Ugandan government met the balance. In the event we were not to be disappointed as, on their first appearance at the Commonwealth Games as an independent team, they distinguished themselves by winning one gold medal and two bronze medals in the boxing events and two bronze medals in the athletics events.

* * *

Early in December 1962, just two months after Uganda Independence Day, a flow of reports was received from West Nile District that tension was rapidly developing between the Congo and the Sudan, which was threatening the territorial integrity of Uganda. Many hundreds of southern Sudanese rebels had sought sanctuary in Orientale Province of the northeastern Congo and were believed to be undergoing military training with the connivance of the Congolese authorities. They were also operating from sympathetic bases, for the Madi Kakwa tribes inhabited both sides of the international border area — a legacy of the late nineteenth-century 'Scramble for Africa'.

The Sudanese army, provoked by several armed raids on convoys and camps in the Congo border area, reacted and mounted a limited penetration of the Congo, burned down several villages and killed some Congolese. Both sides moved up military forces in strength to the tri-junctional area between the Congo, the Sudan and northwest Uganda. The prime minister of Uganda decided to intervene and sent me, as his inspector-general of police, to head a Ugandan government delegation to bring the two warring parties to the conference table.

I was accompanied by the deputy head of Special Branch, Paddy

Erskine, and the local Ugandan district police commander. Erskine and I flew to Arua in one of the aircraft of the Uganda Police Air Wing, piloted by our chief pilot, Chris Treen. I then sent the aircraft to Juba to collect the Sudanese delegation, headed by an old friend of mine, Major General Tahir el Maghboul, who was commandant of Equatoria Province. Tahir and I had met on several occasions in both Kampala and Juba at border security liaison meetings. When the Sudanese delegation arrived we set forth for the Congolese customs post at Vurra on the Uganda–Congo border. The provincial government in Stanleyville, the capital of Orientale Province, had previously been alerted by the government of Uganda that a meeting was proposed, and had agreed to meet the Sudanese under neutral chairmanship, but insisted that the meeting should take place on Congolese soil.

A company of the Uganda Rifles had been moved up, under cover opposite the customs post, on Ugandan territory. When we arrived at the border, General Tahir and I decided to precede the Ugandan and Sudanese delegations on foot and unarmed, as an earnest of our peaceful intentions. Tahir, who was Sandhurst-trained and in full major general's uniform, carried a swagger cane. I was similarly 'equipped'. As we approached the Congolese barrier I asked him if he had any apprehensions as to the reception we would receive, to which he replied to the effect that he had none, as we were only 'dealing with natives'. As it happened, we were met at the border by a Belgian-style Congolese army honour guard, dressed in paratrooper blouses and carrying automatic weapons, which they duly presented. The Sudanese and Ugandan delegations followed.

The venue for this 'international meeting' was a cramped customs building with trestle tables and wooden benches. On arrival, there was no sign of the Congolese delegation, so we waited, having been assured that they were on their way from Stanleyville. We drank tea and smoked cigarettes and waited and waited. An hour and a half later, when we were on the point of abandoning the rendezvous and returning to Arua, a convoy of jeeps drove up in a cloud of dust. The first to dismount and enter the customs post was Manzikala, the 'president' of Orientale Province, representing the central government in Leopoldville

(Kinshasha). Dressed in a green boiler suit and armed with a .45 revolver which dangled between his legs, he was flanked by two Congolese army colonels, both toting sub-machine-guns. General Tahir's and my swagger canes looked puny by comparison.

A platoon of Congolese army troops then took up positions around the customs' post with their weapons trained on us. They looked tense and trigger-happy. Manzikala's initial reaction was one of surprise and suspicion at the Ugandan delegation, which was predominantly European. However, by judicious use of French and Kiswahili (which was understood by the Lingala-speaking Congolese), the ice was rapidly thawed and he accepted my role as intermediary. It was made clear that my brief was to get the Congolese and Sudanese to talk rather than shoot at each other, and General Tahir entered wholeheartedly into the spirit of the meeting.

When it was clear that there was every chance that the Congolese and Sudanese were prepared to discuss their differences amicably, having sworn to eternal African brotherhood, I informed them that I was withdrawing my delegation. To this, General Tahir expressed dismay and tried to persuade us to remain in support. Subsequently, he too withdrew and rejoined us in Arua for a celebratory drink or two before being flown back to Juba. Paddy Erskine and I flew back in the police aircraft to Kampala that evening, arriving at 8.00 p.m., despite a dogleg in the aircraft over the Congo as a result of a navigational error.

Some 12 months later a similar situation developed in the same area, but it was impossible on this latter occasion to get the two sides together, though I personally paid a brief visit to the Sudanese army forward position at Oraba on the Arua–Yei road. I was received with courtesy, but there was no question of parleying with the Congolese. Tension continued between the Sudanese and Congolese until the collapse of the rebel revolt in the eastern Congo early in 1965.

* * *

There was a resurgence of violence, which was now becoming chronic, in the Bakonjo/Baamba counties of Toro, and large numbers of police and military reinforcements had yet again to be drafted into the area. It was now necessary to employ the field tactics of 'search and destroy' against armed gangs, particularly of Bakonjo, who were on the rampage in the Ruwenzori foothills.

* * *

The month was marked by an interesting development in post-independence Buganda. A group of Baganda formed a grass-roots representative movement called *Abawajjere* (common man), which aimed to curtail the powers and privileges of the chiefs and to abolish the *mailo* system of land tenure. It was now evident that ordinary working men and peasants in Buganda were not prepared to tolerate the perpetuation of the semi-feudal nature of local government, and demanded greater representation. It was a movement which clearly met with the approval of the UPC government, though it was careful not to give any indication of overt support for fear of wrecking the UPC/KY alliance. The formation of the movement led to some minor disturbances of little significance.

* * *

Among distinguished visitors to Uganda during the month were Mrs Elspeth Huxley (an old friend who stayed with us), Mrs Golda Meir (the Israeli foreign minister at that time) and Mr Duncan Sandys, the Commonwealth Secretary.

While attempts were being made during the month to iron out some of the difficulties that bedevilled Uganda–Congo relations, particularly the problems of border infringements by the Congolese army and smuggling from the Congo into Uganda of coffee, papain and other products, a visit was made by a high-level Congolese government delegation to Uganda, led by M. Anany, the minister for national defence. I attended a meeting at which he and senior Ugandan ministers agreed on resolutions to restore normal relations and cooperation on all security matters of mutual concern. These were never implemented. It was an interesting exercise in lip service to African unity.

An interesting sidelight to Uganda's proximity to the Congo was the renewal of relations between the Uganda police and the UN Irish contingent. At that time the latter was serving in Katanga Province and, since there were a number of senior officers of Irish extraction in the Uganda police (including myself), we invited two pipers from the Irish army to come to Uganda as our guests ('armed' with their pipes) for our St Patrick's Day celebrations. They played at the police officers' mess and I had the unique privilege of giving a reception at my house with Irish pipers in attendance — much to the envy of other expatriate 'tribal' associations in Kampala.

The summer of 1963 passed relatively peacefully, with the Uganda police able to concentrate on some of the more routine tasks of the force, such as curbing armed robberies and car thefts, which were endemic to the scene. I also took six weeks' leave in Europe between mid-May and the end of June. Early in the month, a party from the Imperial Defence College visited Uganda and we entertained them at the police officers' mess.

* * *

From mid-September the incipient unrest in the southern Sudan assumed the proportions of a full-scale rebellion. Numbers of Sudanese government troops and officials were ambushed and killed by the rebels, operating chiefly in the Torit District. The Sudanese government reacted by mounting a campaign of outright suppression in the south. Most of the victims were innocent civilians, for the Sudanese army tended to operate only on main roads and had little heart to take the fight to the rebels in the bush. All borders between the Sudan and Uganda were closed, with only that at Nimule (on the Nile) remaining open for the use of official and essential supplies traffic, under convoy arrangements made by the Sudanese army.

Clearly, there was a need for much closer consultation between the two governments. Thus, in the first few days of October, I was again entrusted by the prime minister to lead a Ugandan government delegation of administrative and police officers at a liaison meeting held in Juba, Equatoria Province. The main achievement of the meeting was to ensure closer cooperation between the authorities on both sides of the border and agreement that the Uganda security forces should check unauthorized incursions by Sudanese army personnel into Uganda in hot pursuit of rebels. This agreement was contingent on a great degree of security on the Uganda side of the border. Police Special Force units were moved up to the international border area in West Nile District on the west bank of the Nile and in Acholi on the east bank. In addition, new police posts were established in the border area in both districts.

* * *

The first anniversary of Uganda's independence was celebrated with parades and receptions on 9 October 1963; and Sir Walter Coutts, the governor-general, departed. The Kabaka of Buganda was appointed the first president of Uganda by the national assembly and moved into State House, Entebbe.

Meanwhile, throughout October and November the rebellion in the southern Sudan and the disturbances in the Ruwenzori area continued unchecked and imposed a considerable strain on Uganda's security forces. On Obote's instructions, the Uganda army was deployed in strength in support of the Police Special Force units. This was a mixed blessing because, although the hard-pressed police units welcomed relief, the army was so badly disciplined that deployment in the field immediately led to a mass of complaints of robbery, looting and rape — which had to be investigated by the police.

Idi Amin had by then become a battalion commander and such was his ignorance of field tactics that on one joint operation in the Ruwenzori I had to give him a lesson in map reading before his units were deployed in the field. There were still a number of seconded British army officers serving in the Uganda forces, but, with the emphasis on 'Africanization', most operational commands were assigned to newly promoted NCOs who had little or no idea of man-management or tactics. The rot had set in, and a once proud and efficient regiment was rapidly developing into an unprofessional rabble.

✻ ✻ ✻

Both Zanzibar and Kenya attained independence during the month. My wife and I were invited by the government of Kenya to attend the celebrations in Nairobi as guests. We were the only European official guests, and were accommodated at the Norfolk Hotel for the four-day official programme. Among other guests at the hotel were Joshua Nkomo, the Revd Ndabaningi Sithole, various Ugandan government ministers and Harry Belafonte (who, with Miriam Makeba, performed at the state ball). The arrangements were excellent and the crowds enormous.

At the civic reception, held outdoors in the middle of the day in the blazing heat, Humphreys Luande, the leading Ugandan trade unionist, whom I knew well, lurched towards me, very much the worse for wear, with Dr Waiyake, the Kenyan foreign minister-designate, in tow, and insisted on introducing me as 'Mike Macoun, my good friend, who is a "common man" like us.' This I took as a marked compliment and countered by saying, 'Yes, but you have no idea how very common I can be.' It was all great fun and both my wife and I thoroughly enjoyed the experience.

✻ ✻ ✻

We were to return to Uganda to find Kampala seething with rumours of Ugandan government indignation at the conduct of a large party of Europeans at a reception on the night of Kenya's independence. This took place at a private house on Tank Hill on the outskirts of Kampala, where 'the shedding of the white man's burden' was to be celebrated. Although privately organized, a number of European government officials, including three middle-ranking police officers, attended. Apart from a good deal of heavy drinking, charades were performed, including one of a white *bwana* leading a 'black woman' by a rope round her neck. Needless to say, the barmen and waiters were Ugandan Africans, and they, and the government of Uganda, did not appreciate the rather childish and tactless humour of the participants.

Feelings ran high in African circles and on 20 December, on a motion introduced by a backbencher, the incident was debated in the National Assembly. Together with senior African police officers, I attended the debate in the public gallery, and it was all too clear that we were in for trouble. The House condemned the event as blatantly racist and insulting to Africans. This led to a violent anti-European reaction such as had never been witnessed in Uganda before, and to widespread threats and intimidation.

Bill Buse, the manager of the local English-language newspaper, the *Uganda Argus*, was kidnapped, assaulted and humiliated in Kampala market by UPC 'youth wingers' (he was made to carry a bundle of bananas on his head while being subjected to taunts, blows and abuse); the house in which the Tank Hill party had been held was burnt to the ground (the only casualties being two dogs); and the European club at Lira, Lango (Obote's home district) was likewise set on fire.

Full-scale mobilization of all police forces in the Kampala and Entebbe areas took place, and the five organizers of the party were deported without compensation at short notice; all government officials (including the three European police officers) who attended were dismissed and ordered to leave the country forthwith. Anti-European agitation continued until after the New Year and rumours of resignation of senior officials (including myself) were rife. Such was the irrationality of the situation that a rumour was circulated that my wife and I had attended the party, despite the fact that it was common knowledge that we were in Nairobi at the time as guests of Jomo Kenyatta at Kenya's independence celebrations.

There was a great deal of nervous tension in the European community and a number of wives received anonymous telephone calls threatening reprisals. When I attended an evening party at a friend's house and two burglars broke into one of the bedrooms, apart from taking up the chase and driving off the robbers (who were armed with pangas) with a well-directed shot with a heavy brass pot, which came to hand, a 999 call to the central police station brought a whole unit of the heavily armed Police Special Force to the scene — on the grounds that it was believed that I, as inspector-general of police, was the target of an armed attack.

A number of prominent UPC youth wingers were, as a result of the disturbances, arrested and subsequently convicted of assault and given prison sentences. Later, in 1964, they all enjoyed free pardons granted by the government — obviously on political grounds. Thus, for a second time in three years, the year ended with the police force mobilized and I 'celebrated' Christmas and New Year's Eve in uniform.

* * *

These were almost certainly the most eventful and taxing months during my six years as inspector-general of police in Uganda. With the aftermath of deteriorating race relations as a result of the Tank Hill party, in the first few days of the new year we were faced with a major crisis on the Uganda–Rwanda border in Ankole District. As already mentioned, there were in the Tutsi refugee camps, in southwest Uganda, groups of armed militant Tutsi who were bent on raiding their former homeland. The Inyenzi (cockroaches) had obtained possession of smuggled arms from the Congo and planned a large-scale invasion of Rwanda. However, thanks to good intelligence obtained by the Uganda Police Special Branch, the Rwanda authorities had been warned in advance.

The 'invasion' took place on the night of 1–2 January 1964, and approximately 500 men armed with guns and spears took part. Two platoons of the Rwanda Garde nationale awaited them in ambush positions, held their fire until they were on Rwanda territory and then decimated them. At least 200 dead were left to rot as a warning against any future would-be invaders. Many were taken prisoner and released within sight of the Ugandan security forces in position on the international border and mown down with automatic fire as they ran for sanctuary in Uganda. The next day I visited the Kamwezi area, where we had established a temporary border control post manned by a unit of the Special Force, and was horrified to see the whole of the shallow valley on the Rwanda side swarming with vultures. Flocks of vultures had settled on the corpses and, apart from those who had died on the Uganda border, we were unable to intervene and remove the dead. There were no more attempts at invasion by the Tutsi refugees.

There was a new influx of refugees from this action and other reprisals against Tutsi which took place inside Rwanda, and the refugee population in Uganda was swelled by another 5000, mostly women and children. Following upon these events, the Ugandan government belatedly decided to move all the remaining 7000 refugees on the Rwanda border to resettlement areas further north in Toro and western Buganda.

✳ ✳ ✳

News of the Zanzibar coup reached Uganda when the new republic was only five weeks old. Details of the revolt were obtained from the radio network of the White Fathers' Mission in Uganda.

A week later, the whole of East Africa was astounded to learn that the Tanzanian army had mutinied and that President Nyerere had fled the capital, Dar es Salaam. This and the second army mutiny a few days later, in Tabora, have been well documented by many eye-witnesses, so I will not attempt to add to the factual record. It may be of interest, however, to note that we in Kampala, many hundreds of miles away, were kept informed in detail on events, chiefly through Roman Catholic White Father channels. At one stage, when little was known of Nyerere's whereabouts, we were able to obtain accurate information, through mission channels, not only of his 'sanctuary' but also of his state of mind.

Clearly, events in neighbouring Tanzania were of great concern to the government of Uganda and immediate security precautions were taken, including the closure of the international border. All sailings by the Lake Victoria steamers were prohibited and I was authorized by Obote to 'impound' the RMS *Victoria* and the SS *Sybil*. It was the only time in my police career I seized two ships! The RMS *Victoria*, the flagship of the East African Railways and Harbours fleet on the lake, had a full complement of passengers, including a group of American tourists bound for Mwanza in Tanzania.

When I arrived at Port Bell where the ships were moored, I was accompanied by a unit of armed special force police, and we boarded and secured both vessels. Apart from considerable indignation on the part of the captains of both ships, there was alarm among the passengers at being placed under armed guard. I had to address passengers and crew in both instances to reassure them

The author as a student in Munich, Germany, 1933.

The author on first arrival in Dar es Salaam, September 1939.

LEFT. The "ELIE FUSIANI". Free French escapees from Vichy. French-occupied Madagascar.

BELOW. The FANY contingent in Dar es Salaam 1940. The author's wife, Geraldine astride her bicycle in the centre, 1940.

Geraldine and Michael during the year of their marriage, 1940.

ABOVE. Farewell group of Uganda Police wives prior to author's departure, October 1964.

BELOW. The author as Inspector General of Police on visit to Rwanda border after the massacre of Tutsi by Hutu, 1964.

ABOVE. The author inspecting Guard of Honour of the British Solomon Islands Police, 1968.

LEFT. Roy Henry, the Commisioner of Police in Fiji, greeting the author on an inspection visit.

ABOVE. The author as overseas Police Adviser FCO inspecting Police Guard of Honour on arrival in St. Kitts, Eastern Caribbean.

BELOW. Commissioner of Police George Akaola and King Toupou of Tonga.

that I was acting under the orders of the prime minister and that the action had been taken for their safety. Ironically, by the time the ships had been released and were safely in Mwanza, we had an army mutiny on our hands in Uganda. There was also a small group of European women and children who sought sanctuary in Uganda overland from Bukoba in West Lake District in Tanzania. They, in turn, were trapped in Kampala when the Ugandan army mutinied. Among them were a police friend's wife and children who came to stay with us until things quietened down in Tanzania. Coming from a small upcountry station she was delighted to go shopping in Kampala; however, the mutiny spread to the Ugandan army and Geraldine and other police wives spent the night by the telephone waiting for news while I monitored the situation from my headquarters. After the British Army, the Staffords and the Scots Guards, had taken over the airport, I rang home to say I would be bringing a number of officers for supper — we eventually arrived at about 2.00 a.m.

* * *

Ever since independence at the end of 1962, a general and progressive deterioration in standards and discipline in the Ugandan army was discernible. Colonel Cheyne, the army commander at independence, and several of his senior officers had returned to their parent regiments, only to be replaced by seconded British officers, who, for the most part, were unfamiliar with African troops. At the same time, in the interests of 'localization', a number of Ugandan African officers had been commissioned. Some of these officers were young men with good academic qualifications but little or no experience of soldiering or man-management. They had virtually no control over their older NCOs, some of whom had either seen war service or had had operational experience during the Mau Mau rebellion in Kenya. There was also considerable dissatisfaction among the rank and file of the army at their pay and conditions of service. A further disruptive factor was the interference and over-familiarity exercised by certain Ugandan government ministers with their tribal relatives in the army.

73

The minister of internal affairs, Felix Onama, who was in charge of both the defence forces and the police, had assured me on a number of occasions that he kept in close touch with all ranks in the army. He certainly was known to spend Saturday nights in the sergeants' mess in Jinja. The scenario was such that anything could happen, and it did.

The government decided to make a salaries award to the army, starting with officers and NCOs; the rank and file were informed that their award would follow in due course. On 23 January 1964, when reports were received that the barracks in Jinja were in turmoil at the delay on the pay award to the troops, Onama decided to visit the barracks 'to talk to the boys'. I suggested we provided him with an escort, but he brushed the idea aside, stating that he knew his men and that they would listen to him.

He was due for a rude awakening. On entering the cantonment after having been driven to the gates of the barracks, Onama was seized by soldiers who abused him, tore his shirt, kicked him up the backside and then trundled him off to the guard room. News of this outrage was immediately passed to police headquarters in Kampala and I informed the prime minister of the minister's fate. He forthwith summoned the Cabinet in Entebbe. I ordered the police in Jinja to keep a close watch from outside the barracks on developments but not to intervene.

In the meantime, we were being fed by regular 'situation reports' from within the barracks by the British adjutant, who remained in his headquarters' office and was in direct RT contact with the police operations room in Kampala. The situation had now developed into a full-scale mutiny; troops from the headquarters and 'A' companies had mutinied and the cantonment was in chaos. Predictably, the mutineers' first targets were the canteen and liquor store and, before long, most of them were drunk. In the circumstances this was a blessing in disguise, for a large quantity of small arms and ammunition had just been delivered and, in the absence of ready space in the armoury and ammunition store, was standing in the open under tarpaulins.

Onama was held captive in the guard room until the pay claim had been extracted from him by force. The prime minister then sent a group of three ministers — Obwangor, Magezi and Kirya

— to Jinja to parley with the mutineers and obtain Onama's release. This they succeeded in doing, but the mutineers refused to return to barracks until they had the additional cash in hand.

In the meantime, six Police Special Force units, armed with Bren guns, Sterling guns and small arms, were moved up to secure the road and rail bridges over the Nile at Jinja to prevent an armed break-out by the mutinous soldiers. I also gave instructions for the 10-ton bullion van, which was used for the safe custody of cash in transit, to be overturned on the eastern approach road to the Nile bridge, thus effectively blocking the main road to Kampala. This caused considerable dislocation of all east–west road traffic and I was bombarded by complaints from the commercial community. I reminded them that there was little point in keeping the main road open to threats of attack by armed mutineers.

By now, both the police and prison services were placed on 24-hour stand-by. I convened a meeting of 500 police in the central barracks at which I explained the gravity of the situation and reminded them all of their loyalty both to the rule of law and to the government. The police force responded to a man, with one notable exception — a nephew of the minister, who deserted, and was promptly traced, arrested and, after a disciplinary hearing, dismissed from the force without benefits.

The Ugandans in the police force deserve the greatest credit for their conduct during this crisis, for they were being asked to contain an armed mutiny with force of arms, if necessary, where they would be required to fire on their fellow tribesmen or close relatives. All operational units were placed under African command and the remaining expatriates in the force continued to serve in a support role. The force operations room in police headquarters, Kampala, was placed on a 24-hour emergency basis, and automatic weapons were issued to all gazetted officers and inspectors, in case there was a break-out and attack by the mutineers on Kampala and Entebbe. This was necessary, for reports were coming in of threats from Jinja to march on Entebbe to confront the prime minister and the government.

During the afternoon, the situation in the Jinja barracks deteriorated rapidly and all British army officers were withdrawn to quarters, where they and their families were virtually the mutineers' prisoners. Speedy relief action was required before the situation became out of hand. The permanent secretary for internal affairs, Michael Davies, and I were in constant communication with the prime minister in Entebbe and we kept him informed of the situation. He was told bluntly that he had three options:

- To let the mutiny take its course, in which case there would be a serious armed threat to his government;
- to authorize the police force to open fire on and contain the mutiny in the event of a break-out from the barracks, in which case he would have to accept the political consequences of Ugandan killing Ugandan (many of the army and police came from the same tribal areas and there were many close relatives in both services); or
- to call for assistance from the British government. (The 24th brigade was stationed in Kenya and was available at short notice.)

At 6.30 p.m. Milton Obote, the prime minister, decided, rather reluctantly, to exercise the third option. However, he was pressed to hasten because the request for assistance to the high commissioner, Sir David Hunt, would have to be relayed to the British government before the 24th brigade could be authorized to move. It had already been notified of the probability of this plea for outside assistance, so was preparing to move when the go-ahead was approved by London.

The prelude to the operation was conducted in secret and, apart from the prime minister and two or three of his most trusted ministers and senior officials, the British high commission and the permanent secretary and myself, no one was aware that British troops had been alerted to assist in disarming and disbanding the mutinous companies in Jinja. While I remained continuously with my operations staff in police headquarters, I sent a small 'reception committee' under an assistant commissioner to Entebbe to await the relief force, and kept in constant touch with the prime minister's office, the British high commission and Jinja.

Shortly before 11.00 p.m. Hercules troop-carrying aircraft began landing at Entebbe airport. The Minister of Information,

Nekyon (who was Obote's first cousin), Major James Houston, the Uganda Rifles' brigade major, and a senior Uganda police officer were there to 'receive' the troops. Their disembarkation from the aircraft was so speedy, and they were so well rehearsed for situations of this nature, that the 'platform party' were nearly knocked off their feet. The airport was secured within minutes, with British troops in the control tower, in the terminal building and at all entry points to the airport. Police guards, posted earlier on security duties, dropped their rifles and fled, such was their surprise.

The intervention force, under the command of Lieutenant Colonel Dick Stuckey of the Staffords, comprised three companies of the Staffordshire Regiment and the 'right flank' company of the Scots Guards. The Scots Guards, much to their chagrin, were assigned to the task of airport security, while one company of the Staffords embussed on government transport and were on their way to Kampala within half an hour. In the meantime, once it was known publicly that British troops had landed in Uganda, we were able to put contingency plans in hand for accommodation and victualling. By the time Colonel Stuckey and the advance party had arrived at police headquarters in Kampala, the police officers' mess had been reorganized to accommodate the Staffords' forward company, and the mess manageress had been roused from bed and asked to purchase supplies from neighbouring shops (all closed for the night) so that the troops could be given a square meal on arrival. They had left Nairobi at such short notice that they had not had an evening meal. The local shops (mostly Asian) opened without demur and there was a brisk trade in eggs, sausages, potatoes and bacon. A number of European women volunteers were roused from their beds to help with the catering. The general effect in all communities was one of undisguised relief.

Colonel Stuckey and his senior officers were briefed on arrival in the small hours of the morning. It was decided to hold fire for 24 hours in order to bring up the two operational companies and regroup, and to give the mutineers time to surrender. Colonel Stuckey retired to my house and we both had a late dinner cum breakfast and put in a few hours' sleep.

We were greeted in the morning with news of the second Tanzanian army mutiny in Tabora. By then, we were not primarily concerned with events in neighbouring countries, for we had a crisis on our doorstep which required early and quick resolution. There was no indication from Jinja that the mutineers were prepared to surrender; the situation was still very tense and there were fears that they would break out and loot the town, or attack their British officers and families.

Operational planning went ahead. The two additional operational companies of the Staffords were brought up from Entebbe and moved into a Uganda army camp site near Kampala. It was decided to move in during the early hours of 25 January, with the Uganda Police Special Force units in support. The night of 24/5 January saw a steady build-up of troops and police on the west side of the Nile bridges at Jinja.

At 5.00 a.m. on 25 January the combined forces moved in; most of the mutineers were caught in their barracks, many of them drunk, and to a man were overpowered, disarmed and placed in custody. Some 450 soldiers were involved and the operation was carried out without a hitch or bloodshed. It was stated afterwards that the only blood spilt was when a drunken mutineer failed to respond when arrested and was prised from his bed at the point of a bayonet (which broke the skin on his chest). Once the cantonment was brought under control it was essential to clear the camp of the mutineers and their families as quickly as possible.

The ringleaders were arrested, charged with mutiny and transferred forthwith to the central prison at Luzira, near Kampala, to await court martial. The rest of the mutineers were paraded *en masse*, stripped of their badges of rank and dismissed on the spot. It was decided to remove them all, together with their families (a total of 3000 men, women and children), that day. With the prime minister's authority, I commandeered all public and private transport I could lay my hands on and dispatched them all to their home districts. By nightfall there was not a single mutineer left in Jinja. On returning to their homes in disgrace, many of the soldiers were dealt with severely by their ex-soldier fathers, and we heard of a number of cases of parental floggings. Sadly, six months later, due to political expediency on the part of the Ugandan government, most of the mutineers were pardoned and reinstated in the army — thus providing yet another contributory factor to the collapse of military standards and discipline in the Ugandan army so evident ever since.

During the next few days all the arms at Jinja were removed and placed under British Army custody in Entebbe, where the Staffords were to be based for the next seven weeks. While elements of the 24th brigade were tidying up in the aftermath of the Ugandan army mutiny, the 11th battalion of the Kenya Rifles mutinied at Lanet barracks just outside Nakuru in Kenya. This mutiny was promptly suppressed, again with the assistance of the British Army, and there were only two (Kenyan Army) fatalities.

The East African army mutinies at the beginning of 1964 had a profound effect not only on the climate of security but also on confidence in the future stability of these newly independent countries. Probably more important, in the immediate term, was the effect they had on the attitudes of the East African leaders towards the continuing British presence in the public services and the forces of law and order. Non-alignment became a more urgent and positive stance, and the shameful necessity to call on the armed forces of the former colonial power to save the three governments from possible anarchy and disaster resulted in a reaction that manifested itself in an acceleration of Africanization in the civil service, police and army in the shortest possible time. Although there were many who believed that there was a common factor in all three mutinies, which followed one upon the other in a matter of a week, there was certainly no overall plan.

I believe that, with the relaxation of strict military discipline and the heady atmosphere of independence, the African soldier, with the power of the gun in his hand, was prepared to employ the threat, if not the use, of the gun to obtain his objectives, whether these were for better pay or naked political power. The soldiers' loyalty had primarily always been to the regiment or to individual British officers, and not to the state. Training to serve the King or Queen — a remote concept — was in reality training to serve the corporate body of the army. Unlike the police service, which had its roots in loyalty to the concept of the rule of law and service to the community, the armies had no tangible allegiance other than to themselves. Even prior to the mutiny in Uganda, many African officers and NCOs openly stated that they only obeyed 'KAR law'. In addition, power-hungry African politicians cultivated the rank and file of the army as a political power base. The lesson of the mutinies was lost on those same politicians who, instead of ensuring that the armies were kept small and retained a positive defence or border-control role, indulged in one-upmanship with their neighbours. As a result, the armies, particularly Uganda's, became inflated and uncontrollable. I would suggest that the mutinies can best be described as a chain reaction resulting from general malaise and declining standards in the three armies.

* * *

After the withdrawal of British forces from the three East African countries, Tanzania called on Nigeria to provide a peace keeping force for six months while its own army was reorganized. Uganda retained her British officers until 1 July 1964, when the Ugandan government decided to replace overnight all British officers with Ugandans (Idi Amin was appointed Chief of Staff). Kenya initiated a phased withdrawal of British officers from the army, and by the time of the first anniversary of her independence (December 1964), all that remained was a British military training mission. This reaction was reflected in other branches of the public service where the pace of localization was markedly speeded up.

So far as Uganda was concerned, the honeymoon was over; the gradual and progressive withdrawal of expatriate personnel was at an end and a new politically inspired urgency was detectable in plans for 'Ugandanization'. New fears and suspicions were evident and were reflected in political intrigue and jockeying for positions of power. It may be said that with the defection of the armies a new and uncertain chapter in post-independence history opened.

Lee Kuan Yew, the prime minister of Singapore, paid a state visit to Uganda and I met him at the prime minister's reception.

The emergency in Toro continued, with suffering and destruction on a formidable scale. In the absence of a political solution, which would have involved the separation of the two Bakonjo/Baamba counties from the Kingdom of Toro (the UPC power base in the west), the intertribal fighting continued unabated.

✳ ✳ ✳

As the end of the month marked 18 months of independence, I honoured my undertaking to Obote to give six months' notice of intention to retire before the second anniversary of Independence Day. Initially, this was met by polite noises about possibly extending my appointment into 1965, but when it was pointed out that my Ugandan deputy, Erinayo Oryema, had been understudying me as inspector-general of police ever since independence, I was asked to hand over to him as soon as possible.

It was made clear that the government wished to retain my services in an advisory capacity until October and I was asked to state my 'terms'. I said that I was perfectly willing to remain but that I would wish to retain my house, staff car and driver, and have priority use of aircraft in the Police Air Wing for whatever duties I would be required to perform. This was readily agreed and I was then asked to designate my role of adviser. In the first place, it was agreed that, although I would be available in police headquarters for consultation, it would be unfair to my successor, Oryema, to act as his personal adviser. Thus, my role should be that of Chief Adviser of Police to the Minister of Internal Affairs (a rather grandiose title). This involved regular 'commuting' to the ministry in Entebbe, some 20 miles away. However, with a staff car and driver, I was able to do much of my reading of files *en route*. Advantage was taken of my availability to give the permanent secretary, MIA, Michael Davies, a leave break of a few weeks during which I acted as PS to the minister in Entebbe, commuting daily.

For the next six months, whenever there was any situation or crisis which required an on-the-spot appreciation, I was regularly engaged in flying to various parts of the country in my new, very interesting and non-executive role.

✳ ✳ ✳

Refugees from the fighting in the southern Sudan started to flock into Uganda and within weeks topped the 12,000 mark. Temporary camps had to be established in the Kidepo valley in northern

Karamoja to accommodate them and, yet again, the government of Uganda was saddled with the burden of feeding and protecting them.

* * *

In the same month, the communist-inspired and -supported uprising in the eastern Congo started. The area of Uvira in northern Kivu was soon under rebel (Mulelist) control. The revolt in the eastern Congo had now spread to the Kivu and Orientale provinces bordering Uganda, and all western border Ugandan police posts were reinforced. As we had excellent intelligence contacts in the area, we were able to keep both the Ugandan government and the British and American missions in Kampala informed on developments. Some American missionaries who had refused to be evacuated to Uganda in 1960 had to pay the ultimate price for their folly. One particularly horrific consequence of this religious stubbornness was the case of the teenage daughter of an American mission couple who was abducted by the rebels, used as a 'camp follower' for several weeks and finally killed in the Ituri Forest area. Her parents were shot dead before her abduction.

* * *

The revolt in the Ruwenzori took a turn for the worse in large-scale reprisals by the Batoro on the Bakonjo/Baamba communities in their midst. There was wanton killing, including that of women and children. Hundreds were injured. With unrest on the Congo border, intertribal fighting in Toro and vast numbers of refugees from both Rwanda and the southern Sudan, the Ugandan security forces were fully stretched. At no time during this period did I have more than one out of nine Police Special Force units in reserve; the rest were operationally committed.

* * *

In the middle of the month, we were faced with a major security and ceremonial commitment in the state visit of the Emperor of

Ethiopia, Haile Selassie. There was the usual round of parades, state drives, receptions and a state dinner, which my wife and I attended. The Emperor was generous in his disbursement of honours to Uganda's politicians and senior civil servants, and the order of Menelik and the Lion of Judah were freely displayed. It was rather like a Christmas party.

* * *

An international conference between Uganda, Tanzania and Burundi was held in Kampala on the redistribution of the refugees from Rwanda, who now numbered 150,000, and from the southern Sudan (now 15,000). Little was achieved.

From mid-July onwards, there was a complete collapse of Congo central government authority in the country's eastern provinces of Kivu, North Katanga, Maniema and Orientale. Rebel bands controlled all the main centres and there was wanton murder and destruction over wide areas. Those Europeans who had remained were the prime targets and an evacuation plan was implemented, though, as stated earlier, many missionaries remained, despite advice to the contrary, and were to pay the ultimate penalty in the ensuing months.

A steady flow of European refugees, mostly Greeks and Italians, entered Uganda, as did many Congolese central government officials and others who were sympathetic to the Tshombe government in Leopoldville. The rebellion and counterattacks had spread further north and both Paulis and Stanleyville were under direct threat from rebel bands. Numerous engagements took place on the Ugandan border and, because they threatened to involve local communities, large numbers of Ugandan troops and police were moved up to contain the situation.

In the meantime, a counter-campaign was being waged by European mercenaries employed by the Leopoldville government, and this inevitably added a further dimension of savagery to the fighting. Whole communities were slaughtered in the crossfire and a large swathe of the eastern Congo became a battleground. Eventually, the central government troops and mercenaries gained the upper hand, but only at appalling cost to human life.

* * *

An Israeli Air Force training team arrived in Uganda after having been declared *persona non grata* by Tanzania — they were to suffer the same fate at Amin's hands eight years later. There were already Israeli Army and police training personnel in the country who integrated well with the remaining British officers in their duties.

* * *

This was to be my last month in Uganda and, having assisted in the reception and briefing of a party from the Imperial Defence College in London, I took two weeks leave in Kenya. I had already eased out of active commitment to the Ugandan security scene, and decided to have a final break at the coast with my family. On our return, we had to brace ourselves for a final round of farewell parties. Among the numerous ones we attended was a 'concert' given for us by the African constables' wives and the African welfare assistants. It lasted for over three hours and contained some sketches in which the wives wore their husbands' uniforms to perform exaggerated takeoffs of how they were treated by them — in many cases in front of the husbands in question.

It should be said that my relations with the Ugandan government remained cordial to the end and I left with goodwill on all sides. Receptions were given by my minister, Felix Onama, and the police, and I received a silver-plated tea and coffee set contributed to by all ranks of the Uganda police. I left Uganda with sadness but without regrets. The time was already overdue for Ugandans to manage their own affairs and the force was now in able, professional and dedicated hands. The real tragedy of Uganda was to come, and many of those Ugandan officers with whom I had worked over the previous six years were to become victims of Amin's tyranny.

* * *

The catalogue of violence, reflected in the foregoing account of events covering the prelude to independence and its immediate aftermath, requires analysis. It cannot be dismissed lightly, nor can it be considered typical of the process of decolonization.

Why, in a country blessed with abundant natural resources, higher educational standards than all its neighbours and ample financial reserves, should there be almost constant internecine strife, often of the utmost brutality, together with an annual homicide rate only surpassed by the United States? It will be clear from the record of the years 1959–64 that barely a month passed without some new crisis or a new outbreak of violence in areas of chronic instability. This state of almost constant tension placed an enormous burden on the Uganda police, yet we were able, despite frequent disruption, to carry out a localization programme which was the envy of all our neighbours in East and central Africa.

Man's inhumanity to man is, as we all know, not peculiar to Africa, but in Uganda — much more so than in either Tanzania or Kenya (Mau Mau apart) — it appeared to be endemic within the community. Sociologists may well ascribe this to the horrifying feudal sanctions imposed on the people in the old kingdoms; there may be a point here, without indulging in generalization, for violence and cruelty were much worse and more widespread in the Bantu areas of the country. (A worthwhile subject for academic research?) It is probably fair to say that intertribal, religious and political differences within the community compounded the fragmentation of 'The Pearl of Africa'. The protectorate government, in the run-up to independence, was faced with an almost insuperable task of reconciliation.

The independence constitution, despite built-in safeguards, was unsatisfactory because it attempted to reconcile parliamentary democracy with traditional semi-autonomy in the kingdoms. When Iain Macleod visited Uganda in September 1960, it was suggested that a Westminster-style constitution would not work. He accepted the dilemma but said that we knew it could work and that we could not bequeath anything else. Yet, had the British government taken an unusual (and probably unacceptable) gamble in insisting on a central government with undisputed control over local (kingdom) authorities, it is possible that Uganda might have been spared some of the agony of post-independence strife.

Even Obote's concession in 1963 in appointing the Kabaka as a non-executive president failed, for the Baganda continued to conspire against the established constitutional authority of the state — through State House. The crunch came and the Kabaka was obliged to flee the country, leaving in his wake many thousands of Baganda who fell to the reprisals of the army. Significantly, the officer in charge of the troops who stormed the Twekobe (the Kabaka's palace) on Mengo Hill was none other than Colonel Idi Amin. The bloody history of Uganda since the army coup of 1971 has been well documented and is known to the world.

* * *

I revisited Uganda twice after my departure from the country in October 1964: once in July 1971 and again in May 1979. On the first occasion, it was a few months after Amin's seizure of power when, as a result of the rather naïve belief by the then British government that Amin was better for Uganda and us than Obote, I participated in a two-man police/military aid mission to evaluate the areas and scale of British aid that could be given to the Ugandan police and armed services. My partner in what proved to be a largely abortive exercise was Colonel James Houston, who was the last British army officer to leave the country in 1964.

We spent ten days in Kampala, during which I met the acting president, Colonel Obitra-Gama (Amin was in London on an official visit during which he was entertained by Her Majesty the Queen), and senior Ugandan government officials, as well as all the senior police officers. There was no commissioner or deputy commissioner, and the vice-president suggested that I used my old office, which I had vacated on retirement seven and a half years previously. I found the police force in a state of disarray and unable to carry out its statutory duties. Leaderless and demoralized, it was a very different force from the one I had left in 1964. Police officers acted in fear of the army; while I was in Kampala, two CID officers investigating a case of corruption by an army officer were removed from their office by armed soldiers, never to be seen again. The day before I left, a senior detective officer, similarly involved in an inquiry into theft by an army officer, was gunned down by armed off-duty soldiers in broad daylight on the Kitante Road on his way home from work. It was patently obvious that, although the police force desperately needed retraining and material assistance, until the rule of law was restored any assistance would be in vain.

Meanwhile, James Houston was faced with an equally unsatisfactory situation in the armed services. Well-trained professional young officers were being intimidated by NCOs from Amin's own tribal group. The army was divided within itself — West Nile versus the Acholi and Langi (Obote's clansmen and supporters). While we were there outbreaks of fighting between tribal groups were reported in a number of barracks. In these clashes, with heavy casualties, the Acholi and Langi were the principal victims, for the army commanders — predominantly Madi/Kakwa from West Nile District and Nubis ('expatriate' southern Sudanese) — condoned the slaughter. Religious undertones were again evident, for most of Amin's chosen officers were Muslim. By the end of our ten days' abortive mission, some 600–700 soldiers had been killed. Because of the obvious danger of both military training and material aid being given to armed forces that were rent asunder with intertribal rivalries and killings, Houston and I returned to London with firm advice that the £10 million which had been allocated for the rehabilitation and development of the security forces in Uganda had better be set aside. Amin's popularity with the British government was short lived.

✻ ✻ ✻

In May 1979, a month after Uganda had been 'liberated' from Amin's thrall by the Tanzanian army, assisted by soldiers of the so-called Uganda National Liberation Front, I was asked, in my capacity as overseas police adviser in the Foreign and Commonwealth Office, to accompany the acting high commissioner, Dick Posnett, who had just paid a brief visit to London to report on the problems of post-Amin Uganda, on his return to post. My mission was to examine how best HMG could assist in rehabilitating the Ugandan police service so that it could meet its priority task of restoring some semblance of law and order in the country.

On boarding the aircraft at Heathrow, we discovered that Martin Aliker (best man at Obote's wedding and one of President Lule's principal advisers), George Kanyahamba (the attorney-general) and Elizabeth Bagaaya (Princess Elizabeth of Toro), all of whom I had known well in the past, were among our fellow passengers. Both Aliker and Kanyahamba had been on Ugandan government business in London; Elizabeth was returning from exile for a second time. As she was accompanied by a Ugandan journalist, it could only be assumed that she was involved in some 'feature' promotion. I reminded her of our lunch date in 1971 at the Imperial Hotel, Kampala, when the dining-room staff, all of whom were Batoro, greeted her arrival by kneeling and clapping.

Dick Posnett and I spent the morning of our arrival in East Africa at the British high commission in Nairobi, lunched with Sir Stanley and Lady Fingland at their residence in Muthaiga and then chartered a Beechcraft Baron six-seater aircraft after lunch to fly to Entebbe. We flew direct over western Kenya and Lake Victoria and arrived at the new (Amin's) international airport an hour and a half later.

Anti-aircraft guns and foxholes, manned by Tanzanian troops, were much in evidence as we touched down. The apron was littered with the remains of Amin's air fleet: a Grumman Gulfstream executive jet (intact), the notorious Uganda Airways 'whisky-run' Boeing 707 (badly damaged by gunfire, with a collapsed undercarriage), a C130 Lockheed Hercules transport aircraft (serviceable and in use ferrying coffee out of Uganda) and a Fokker Friendship (used by Uganda Airways for the unscheduled Entebbe to Dar as Salaam service).

As we drove through Entebbe we passed Amin's personal helicopter, which had been installed at a road crossing — with local African children using it as a 'playground'. We had been met at the airport by high commission staff and, after clearing immigration without difficulty, drove in convoy — Union Jacks on all vehicles — through three roadblocks, manned by Tanzanian troops, to Kampala, arriving at 5.30 p.m. *En route*, near the village of Kajansi, we passed the scene of the ambush of Colonel Gaddafi's Libyans by Tanzanian troops. It was a perfect ambush position in a cutting on the main Entebbe–Kampala road. The signs of the ambush were still apparent — blackened road surface, burnt-out armoured personnel carriers and trucks. Many Libyans died at the scene.

Outwardly, Kampala appeared unscathed, but on closer examination one could see that every shop and showroom in Kampala Road had been looted and stripped; one or two buildings had been burnt out and no shops had been reopened since 'liberation' a month previously. No replacement stocks had been imported and, at the time of the visit, it was not possible to buy a shirt or even a toothbrush in Kampala. Shortly after my arrival, I gave one of my shirts to a senior Ugandan police officer who was down to his last collarless one. A supply of cheap toilet soap, which I had brought with me, was received by old friends as if it were gold. In addition, as a 'gift of conscience', I returned the plaque bearing the Ugandan coat of arms, which I had when I was inspector-general of police 15 years previously, to the new police commissioner, David Barlow.

Shortly after our arrival in Kampala that evening, Dick Posnett and I visited government headquarters at Nile Mansions in Kampala. In the lobby of the building there was a constant coming and going, with Ugandan exiles (John Kazzora, John Barigye and Miss Kibuka-Musoke, to mention three) mingling with Tanzanian troops, some of whom were teenagers, with their AK47 sub-machine-guns at the ready. The general atmosphere was one of relief combined with uncertainty as to the future.

Because of a lack of accommodation, food and security, I joined the rest of the high commission staff who were camping out at the high commissioner's residence on Nakasero Hill. There were 12 of us in all and the residence was operated as a mess. We had communal feeding — and drinking — until the third day, when the beer ran out and we were 'obliged' to drink Scotch or gin. Fortunately, on the fourth day, the vanguard of the US embassy staff arrived armed with Scotch, wine and apples. They were billeted in the International Hotel (built by Obote on the old Kampala Club tennis court area), but there was no food there other than *matoke* (plantains) or beans and, in any case, much of the hotel was used by the Tanzanian army (and their 'girlfriends') as accommodation, so the Americans decided to join our mess for meals.

Kampala, during those early post-Amin days, was full of heavily armed trigger-happy troops (mostly Tanzanian) and the nights were punctuated with gunfire. It was unsafe to travel in the city after nightfall and a self-imposed curfew existed. There was little to do except talk, read, eat and drink. We had many official visitors during the hours of darkness, including senior police officers who sought relaxation and refreshment, which was generously provided by Dick Posnett.

On the night before I left, the shooting was more or less continuous from 9.30 p.m. until 3.00 a.m. An exchange of automatic fire at the top of the garden, about 100 yards from the residence, made us abandon our star-gazing on the terrace to seek cover behind the concrete walls of the sitting room. During the same night I was woken at 3.00 a.m. when someone fired a mortar bomb in the Kitante valley just below us. There were various theories about who was responsible for the nightly gunfire:

- Tanzanian troops winkling out the remnants of Amin's army (improbable);
- exchange of fire with armed *kondos* (robbers) (possible);
- troops and police shooting stray dogs (most unlikely); or
- bored and drunken Tanzanian troops firing indiscriminately at anything that moved — or at shadows (very likely).

All in all, Kampala was a very hazardous place in which to attempt to pursue any social life at night. The daylight hours were spent at meetings with what remained of the Ugandan police hierarchy, in an attempt to establish priority areas in which HMG could assist. Such was the demoralization and decimation under Amin, followed by a week of wanton destruction and looting by the population of Kampala after his downfall, that every area was a priority one. There was no police transport (most had been taken by Amin's retreating troops); the mechanical workshops had been stripped; the main police stores had been cleaned out except for boxes of medals struck by Amin and three Union Flags (one of which I signed for on loan to the high commissioner's residence, which was flagless); the marine section at Port Bell was without boats; the police training college and police school were without furniture, books or training aids; and the police vote was 'in the red'. Curiously, the police radio workshops and the main tele-communications network remained intact — presumably because no one could either use police radio equipment or sell its spares on the black market.

I visited all the main police headquarters branches in and around Kampala where, despite the appalling lack of resources, there were many officers who had returned from exile or the bush and were anxious to commence the task of reconstruction. Nearly all the remaining senior officers had served with me before I left Uganda in 1964, and I genuinely felt I was among old friends.

On the Friday (25 May 1979) before I left, I received a message from Gilbert Seruwagi, who was acting director of the CID, to the effect that the police had discovered the remains of Mrs Dora Bloch (murdered at the time of the Entebbe raid) in the Kivuvu Forest near Mukono on the Jinja Road (some 17 miles east of Kampala). Arrangements were made by the high commission to send telegrams to London and Tel Aviv, notifying them of the find and asking for forensic assistance from Israel to identify the remains from Mrs Bloch's medical and dental history. There was little left of the poor lady other than a few bones, a half-burnt-out skull and the remaining strands of a nylon stocking.

On my last full day in Kampala, a number of meetings were held in the British high commission with a Crown Agents' team on a visit to Uganda and with American and Swedish embassy staff. Dick Posnett and I spent the afternoon, after 'negotiating' two roadblocks, at the Kanjani Church of Uganda in the Gayaza area some ten miles out of Kampala. The church and school had been rebuilt and we received a warm welcome from the villagers. Life in this rural area appeared to have remained unchanged by the tur-moil in and around the city.

On Sunday 27 May, before leaving Entebbe for Nairobi (again on a charter aircraft), Dick and I had an audience with HE the President, Professor Y. K. Lule, at State House, Entebbe. We dis-cussed the security situation with frankness, and Lule admitted that something of the order of 5000 modern weapons were in unauthorized possession, including 1000 which had been looted from the armoury in Moroto, Karamoja, when Amin's troops fled.

Most of these arms were now in the hands of Karamojong tribes-men, who either used them on cattle raids on their neighbours or traded them across the Kenya border. Lule also stated categori-cally that, apart from military operations against the remnants of Amin's fleeing troops, large numbers of armed criminal elements in the country precluded any early withdrawal of the Tanzanian army. The first step towards restoration of civil order would of necessity have to be combined police/military operations. With a decimated and demoralized police force and an infant ragtag Ugandan army, a limited disarming operation would be difficult to contemplate. Lule also hinted that certain elements in the Uganda National Liberation forces were hostile to the interim regime and planned a restoration of Obote to power. This was to be a well-founded suspicion, as subsequent events proved. We were invited to remain for a light lunch at State House, where we were joined by Professor Semei Nyanzi, one of the presidential advisers. I then left after lunch, for Nairobi and 'civilization'.

The conclusion to this visit was much more constructive than that of 1971. The British government agreed, with a strong recom-mendation from the high commissioner backed by my findings, to give priority aid to the Uganda police as one agency available to the government of Uganda trained and capable of contributing, in the long run, to the restoration of law and order in a totally chaotic and unstable situation. The sum of £1 million was allo-cated to provide for a programme of advanced and specialized training of senior officers in the United Kingdom, for vehicles and equipment, and for instructional aids for police training establish-ments.

Over the next 18 months, some 70 Ugandan police officers, all with experience dating back to pre-independence days, attended command and detective courses in Britain — the majority at the Devon and Cornwall Constabulary Training Centre at Exeter. At the same time, material assistance was given to the expansion and retraining of the force in Uganda.

As is well known, Uganda was not yet out of the wood, and political fragmentation, rivalry and armed anti-government fac-tions continued to militate against any genuine and progressive restoration of stability to the country. It should be remembered that it took over ten years for the Congo to recover from the trauma of post-independence mutiny, civil war and interfactional fighting. Uganda's experience under Amin was that much more tragic; the healing process took longer.

8

Post-Retirement Assignments, Re-Employment and Consultancies: 1965–79

S ome months prior to my departure from East Africa in October 1964, after 25 years' service in Tanganyika, Kenya (war service) and Uganda, I was fortunate enough to be invited by the British Information Service office in New York through the then director, an old friend from school and Oxford days, to undertake a lecture tour of the United States from the west coast to Washington to record my experiences and conclusions on Africa in transition from colonial status to full independence. This was to include optional topics on the situation and role of the forces of law and order, current political and diplomatic developments, post-independence African attitudes and a general forecast on likely post-independence developments in East Equatorial Africa.

Having lived through the prelude to independence in Tanganyika (latterly as deputy commissioner of Pehin, for six months as acting commissioner) and through the changeover and the first two years of an independent Uganda (as the last expatriate inspector-general of police), I readily agreed.

As my wife and I had previously planned to travel to Britain via Australia (where at that time her sister lived), the Far East and North America on our retirement leave, this proved to be an additional bonus, which would enable me to visit no less than 11 different states — California, Arizona, New Mexico, Texas, Arkansas, Missouri, Minnesota, Ohio, Kentucky, Washington DC and New York.

Audiences selected by the BIS New York included branches of the English-Speaking Union, of the Committee on Foreign Affairs and the Council of World Affairs (both local self-supporting associations), 'Town Hall' (Chamber of Commerce) Los Angeles, university study groups and police academies. Television, radio and press coverage was provided at most stopovers. The tour culminated in lectures delivered at the Office of Public Safety, Department of State and a visit to the FBI headquarters in Washington DC, after which I attended a final debriefing session at the BIS office in New York City.

On my return to Britain, after visiting relations in Ottawa, I paid a short flying visit to my elder son who was at that time working for the Anglo-American Corporation in Johannesburg, before catching up with the progress of our younger son at Oxford University. At the same time, I put out feelers for possible post-retirement re-employment.

I had already been approached by the United Nations in New York with an offer to join a multinational police training exercise in Kinshasa, Zaire. This was declined, despite temptingly favourable terms, because I had only just emerged from years in Africa and had no desire to return so soon — particularly to Zaire, with which I had had close contacts while I was in Uganda during the chaos of the years after Congo independence in 1960. Offers of employment were also made in Aden, as an internal security adviser in the run-up to independence there, and as head of the preventive service (customs) in Hong Kong, both of which I declined, preferring to settle down and seek employment in Britain.

After a few months of adjustment to living in the UK after a quarter of a century overseas, I successfully applied for a Home Office post as a civilian lecturer in the Department of General Studies at the National Police Staff College at Bramshill House, Hampshire and entered the quasi-academic field for the first time since my Oxford days. My subjects were international affairs and modern and economic history, and I was assigned to a group of 12 mature police students as a syndicate director on the intermediate command course. They were all sergeants of some years' experience aspiring to become inspectors. They came from various forces in the UK and included an inspector from Dominica in the eastern Caribbean.

The six months at the college exposed me to working in an institutional setting, which I found both novel and stimulating. However, early in 1966, I learned that the post of deputy inspector-general of police at the Colonial Office was to become vacant and, after preliminary enquiries, submitted my application. After being interviewed shortly afterwards, I was delighted to learn that my application had been successful and I was offered the post with effect from 1 April 1966.

Before returning to a post closely associated with overseas policy, I decided in the interim (March 1966) to accept a long-standing invitation to conduct a lecture tour in eastern Canada under the auspices of the Association of Canadian Clubs, whose director, Eric Morse, I had met at the conclusion of my lecture tour of the United States early in 1966. Thus, before taking up my new post as DIG of colonial police, I experienced a new challenge of carrying out a lecture tour of two weeks in Quebec, Ontario Province, Canada. Again, the dominant theme of this tour, as in the USA in 1965, was Africa in transition. I visited Ottawa, Montreal, Shawinigan (Trois Rivières), Quebec City, Arvida (on the Saguenay River–Labrador border), Belleville, Coburg, Sania, Brantford, Chatham, London, Guelph, Lindsay and Port Hope during the two weeks' lecture tour. All in all, it was a very satisfactory and rewarding introduction to eastern Canada with which, in the forthcoming years, I was to have close associations.

On 1 April 1966, I assumed my new post of deputy inspector-general colonial police and, after a year, was promoted to inspector-general, where I remained until my final retirement at the end of 1979. During my tenure of office, the Colonial Office was first absorbed into the newly created Commonwealth Relations Office, which in turn was amalgamated with the Foreign

Office to be redesignated the Foreign and Commonwealth Office. The post of inspector-general colonial police was then redesignated overseas police adviser/inspector-general of police, dependent territories.

The office was a small department of the Foreign and Commonwealth Office and I was supported by a deputy, a staff officer/administration officer and a personal assistant/secretary. We also enjoyed the responsibility of advising the Overseas Development Administration on police training, development support and technical assistance to police forces overseas, both Commonwealth and foreign. (See Appendix G for a more detailed summary of the role and responsibilities of the department.) A British advisory and support service was provided for restructuring, man management and training in specialized and technical fields, and it gave advice on police development projects.

This very broad brief entailed travel overseas by my deputy and myself for an aggregate of three months of every year. In total, we visited 78 different countries and territories, many on a number of occasions, between 1966 and 1979. In addition, I attended no less than 12 Interpol conferences as a member of the United Kingdom delegation. A further commitment was to be available at short notice to travel to areas of incipient disorder, which took me to Sri Lanka, Anguilla, Bermuda, Jamaica, Afghanistan, Mali, Grenada and Uganda.

Thus, towards the end of 1979, after 41 years of association with the British police service at home and overseas, I retired for the third time, but retained a residual interest in a lifetime profession in the ensuing six years of activity (up to 1985), carrying out consultancies for the FCO/ODA in the Caribbean, for the overseas department of the St John Ambulance Association in Africa, as a guest lecturer at the National Police Staff College, as the Secretary of State's representative on the Hong Kong government Police Appointments Board and as a non-executive director of the Control Risks Organization.

9

Overseas Interludes

It should be emphasized that during my 14 years as a police consultant, there were many experiences — some spectacular, some potentially dangerous and others downright bizarre — that should be recorded as a postscript to a catalogue of official duties overseas. Although exacting at times, requiring patience, a sense of fun and some ventriloquism, they could never be described as humdrum. Hence, a final chapter on the lighter and often enjoyable side to an official career which, in the final analysis, embraced some 78 of the countries and territories in the world.

The Queen's last birthday parade before Ugandan independence
Having paraded before the governor, government ministers and various VIPs, the KAR and Uganda police repaired to Government House in Entebbe for the traditional champagne toasts to HM The Queen. Bonhomie was the order of the day and I found myself in the company of Lawrence Ssebalu, a minister in Uganda's internal self-governing Cabinet. He was immaculately dressed in a three-piece suit, sober tie and well-polished shoes. His opening gambit was to the effect that, 'It is good when we chaps can get away from our wives and have a good man-to-man chat.' I readily agreed and, in conversation, ranged freely on male subjects. After three glasses of champagne, he suddenly turned to me and said 'I say, old fellow, do you know where I can break water in this place?' I duly directed him to one of the lavatories assigned to male guests — and lost myself in the crowd.

All in a day's work — Caribbean impressions
This is a miscellany of incidents experienced over a period of 12 years (1967–79) during which I visited all the English-speaking islands of the Caribbean, several on a number of occasions, first as inspector-general of colonial police and later redesignated as the overseas police adviser to the Foreign and Commonwealth Office. After 50 years of neglect there was much work to be done towards modernizing the structure and resources of the islands' police forces, as well as in allocating £4 million of UK aid to the rehabilitation of police buildings and accommodation, and to the provision of transport, telecommunications and instructional aids.

As anyone familiar with the region will know, there was also a fair modicum of time devoted to public relations, which involved social and recreational activities in company with my West Indian hosts, including, on occasions, participation in 'jump-ups'.

The incidents outlined below are what made these visits interesting, entertaining and sometimes startling. On these inspections and consultancy visits I was invariably accompanied by regional police advisers, who, fortunately for me, were, in succession, a fun-loving Irishman, Jimmy Mulligan, known affectionately as 'Slattery's Mounted Foot', and an extrovert Scot called Murdo MacKenzie, thus ensuring that our travels were laced with light-hearted relaxation.

Don't smoke in the shower
On one of my visits to the eastern Caribbean, I arrived tired and dirty at Road Town on Tortola in the British Virgin Islands, retired to my hotel room, stripped down and prepared for a cool refreshing shower. Surprise, surprise, when I turned on the tap, instead of cool fresh water, I was immersed in 100-octane gasoline! This was a mere error of judgement on the part of the hotel room servant who had filled the cistern with gasoline and not H_2O — there is apparently little sense of smell on the island.

Flash Harry and a dog's breakfast
As manager of the hotel 'Flash Harry' was distinguished only by his constant presence at the bar and ability to delegate all executive duties to his staff. Although his hotel was well built, designed

and equipped, maintenance was clearly at a premium, as drains had an uncanny knack of becoming blocked at the most awkward moments and sash cords, when pulled, seemed only to do damage.

Service at breakfast was at a standstill until 'Flash Harry' had emerged, unshaven and with shirt tails flapping, bearing his family dog's breakfast of bones and sliced meat. Whereupon, once the dog had been fed, life and service in the hotel began and 'Flash Harry' resumed his customary position in the bar.

Day-0 in Dominica

Church bells at 5.30 a.m. and the faithful filed in for the Easter retreat. Curtains were drawn and directly beneath my hotel bedroom an elderly female road sweeper hitched up her skirts and relieved herself from the standing position in the yard.

Fasten your seat belts

Accompanied by the commissioner of police, St Vincent, we were airborne in a light aircraft over the Grenadines and were conscious of an ominous banging on the fuselage. After rapid consultation with the pilot, it was realized that one of the seat belts had been shut in the door after take off and the end was playing loose in the slipstream. My travelling companion, the St Vincent police chief, who had somehow ignored his seat belt on takeoff, which was adrift outside the aircraft, then made to open the door in midflight but, just in time, I struck his hand clear. One does not really like to see a good friend depart on a 500-foot 'freefall' into the blue Caribbean.

The flagship

The pride of the Royal St Vincent Police Force was its patrol boat. On one of our seaborne patrols of the outer islands, I heard the cry 'Man, it's busted!' When I asked what was the problem, I was told that the radar, echo sounder and radio were out of order. When smoke started to pour out of the ventilators and through the deck boards, the bland explanation was that the exhaust manifolds had corroded away. A bare foot applied to the deck plates was almost fried on contact but the 'Admiral' (marine superintendent) took no umbrage when he was asked to keep the craft within 200 yards of the nearest shore for easy swimming. All in a day's work!

Caribbean farewell: social culture in the Turks & Caicos Islands
We had spent three days on Grand Turk on a short inspection of police units in the Turks & Caicos Islands. This was the third occasion when Murdo MacKenzie, the regional police adviser, and I had ventured into this colonial backwater and, on each occasion, we encountered the unexpected. Jake Macartney, the chief minister, was a maverick radical who was at home with informality. This boded ill for relations with the colonial governor who was conventional and believed in protocol.

There were problems of drug running. The islands, due to their remoteness, lack of resident population, absence of administration and a small overstretched police force, provided an ideal stopover destination for drug-smuggling by trawlers and other craft from Colombia and Venezuela to Florida from unsupervised island airstrips. With the governor's acquiescence, I arranged to have a man-to-man discussion over several rum punches with Macartney at my hotel. This proved very rewarding and we came to a satisfactory agreement on the necessary countermeasures to deal with the situation.

On completion of official commitments and prior to flying to Miami, Murdo and I decided to have a snack lunch and a beer prior to departure. As the only guests in the hotel, we enjoyed the undivided attention of the staff, with whom we had developed personal and friendly relationships. On announcing our imminent departure, we bade them all farewell and thanked them for their attention. Then, suddenly, the elderly cook appeared with a rush from the kitchen, embraced us both warmly and promptly seized us jointly by our testicles as a final gesture of farewell! When we reached the airport, smarting from this sharp reminder of Turk Islands goodwill, we were introduced to a lady know as 'Peanuts'. She was there to meet the incoming flight from Miami to 'select' likely customers for her hospitality. On enquiring, we discovered that she was the 'Madame' of the local brothel — a lady with foresight and initiative. Grand Turk certainly lived up to its reputation for the unexpected!

Arabian interlude and Aden revisited (1972)

Early in 1972, Edward Heath, the then prime minister, met President Al-Iriani of the Yemen Arab Republic (North Yemen) at the United Nations in New York and was asked if he could send a police adviser to Sana'a, the capital of YAR, to advise his government on what measures could be taken 'to bring the YAR police force into the twentieth century'. On his return, Heath instructed the Foreign and Commonwealth Office to endeavour to meet this somewhat ambitious request. So, as overseas police adviser, I found myself bound shortly afterwards for the Arabian Peninsula.

Initially, I flew Saudi Air ('dry'!) to Jeddah. Fortunately, among the passengers was a kind American lady, the wife of an oil executive, seated across the aisle from me, who, realizing my predicament in having to drink synthetic lemon juice, produced a whisky flask and plied me generously with tots *en route*.

I was met on arrival in Jeddah by Hugh Leach, a first secretary in the British embassy compound. He was to be my companion and escort on our sortie into the Yemen Arab Republic. As he was an ex-officer in the Trucial Oman Scouts and a brilliant Arabist, I could not have been in better company. On arrival at his home, he pointedly led me to his study, which I was free to use for note taking and so forth. To my relief, the book shelves were flanked by an ample supply of hard liquor. My host entertained generously and at a lunch the day after my arrival, he insisted that the male guests disclosed their parent regiments so that he could play the appropriate bugle calls as we entered the dining room singly. After lunch, he entertained us all with music on a harmonium as we took our coffee.

After two memorable days in Jeddah, we flew together in a clapped-out Yemen Air plane to the capital, Sana'a. After a shaky approach and landing at the airport, we were somewhat surprised to learn that air traffic control was in the hands of a 16-year-old schoolboy (who was fortunately literate in English).

The British embassy in Sana'a had only recently been reopened and we were billeted on a young second secretary and his wife. As there was only one bed in the spare room, Hugh elected to sleep on the roof under the stars. After a number of official calls, including one to the deputy president (invariably surrounded by gun-toting soldiers as an escort) we strayed into the old city and visited the souk where I purchased a *jambia* (dagger) from a tribesman (which I have to this day).

We dined one night with the ambassador and also at the so-called Embassy Club (hard liquor available), which seemed to be largely patronized by senior Yemeni officials, who were supposedly 'total abstainers'. The ambassador's dinner party ended up with my host/escort Hugh disappearing into the night with an allegedly 'curfew-bound' Sana'a, determined to make a midnight ascent of a local mountain, the Jebel Nakum, despite entreaties to return home. I was then dispatched to try and locate him, an impossible task, but was greatly relieved when he emerged from the network of side streets to arrest our search vehicle, brandishing a stick. He was persuaded to return home with me and was eventually banished to his overnight pitch on the roof. Two days later, I learned that, because of an outbreak of cholera in the Hodeida area of the Yemen, the Saudis had closed their border.

Having achieved my 'mission' and undertaken to arrange for an experienced British police officer to be sent to the Yemen to reorganize and train a CID, I was at a loss as to how I should return to my base in the UK. This was resolved by the ambassador who assigned an embassy Land-Rover and escort (an émigré Adeni police superintendent) to take me to Aden (overland to Taiz) in the hope of obtaining air transport to Aden or Djibouti. Thus, the last leg of my exodus from Sana'a was assured.

We set out the next morning with my escort and a competent driver on the long leg to the People's Democratic Republic of the Yemen (South Yemen). Our route followed a good dirt road (Anglo-German Development Project) across the high plateau, flanked by mountains up to 12,000 feet high; through the medieval town of Hizyaz; up the Nakil Yaslam escarpment, passing a partially burnt-out Egyptian tank dating from the civil war and now occupied by a herdsman and his family; across the Qaa Jahran plain, where a grounded and wrecked Saudi aircraft lay; on through the towns of Dhamar and Jerim and the Samara mountains, with a network of irrigation canals dating back 1000 years on the slopes of the escarpment; then through two more small towns, Ibb and Kaida, with derelict Turkish forts on the outskirts (a legacy of the Ottoman occupation); and finally to Taiz, the southern capital of the North Yemen. As the verges of the highway were liberally flanked with khat trees, our driver made frequent unscheduled stops to pluck fistfuls of their leaves, which he chewed with apparent satisfaction most of the way.

The setting of Taiz was spectacular with a backdrop of towering cliffs, but the town itself was congested with people and vehicles and most buildings were in a state of disrepair. My police superintendent and I were billeted in a downtown hotel and shared a bedroom. I was granted priority use of the 'loo' as my escort disclosed (disarmingly) that he invariably squatted on the seat. As the water was undrinkable and unsuitable even for cleaning teeth, my escort managed to obtain a bottle of Russian mineral water (from the Caucasus) for our mutual use. The next hurdle was to obtain an air ticket to Aden, my next destination. In this, I was assisted by the Middle East Airlines representative in Aden, Ibrahim Mokbel, whom I had met socially in Sana'a and who was also staying in transit in the hotel.

After an unsuccessful attempt to obtain a booking for the flight to Aden the following afternoon at the Al Yamda (Aden Airways) office, Ibrahim intervened, told me to go to a neighbouring coffee bar and have a *mazbut* — Turkish coffee. He appeared after ten minutes with my onward ticket, stating that I had now, after his intervention, been placed at number two on the passenger list. How so? Well, Ibrahim had offered the travel agent an MEA complimentary airbag and the displaced passenger 20 *rial*s and an assurance that he would be on the next flight.

Knowing that he too wished to join me but had no ticket, he assured me that, as he knew the Al Yamda pilot whom he would meet on arrival, the disbursement of a further 20 *rial*s would ensure that the second displaced passenger would be equally compensated. After a fast-food supper at the so-called American Club (a resthouse on the outskirts of Taiz) I retired to my hotel.

The next morning I was treated to a conducted tour of the deposed imam of Yemen's palace, which was then open as a visitors' attraction. Our guide, a 'good' republican, stressed how decadent the former imam had been, pointing out peepholes overlooking the approach to his sanctuary so that he could select young male visitors as 'companions' and the false bottom of the imam's Koran case which concealed a bottle of Gordon's gin.

After lunch, I jointed my Middle East Airlines friend, Ibrahim Mokbel, at Taiz airport and awaited our connecting flight to Aden. The aircraft duly arrived, we claimed our tickets and then boarded the place. I noticed that some of the wing spars were secured with DIY twine and, as the only non-Arab on board, I settled down to the short 40-minute flight to Aden. However, on discovering that my seat belt was defective — one strap being a piece of discarded British Army webbing — I summoned the captain, who assured me that all I needed to do was to loop the unmatching straps and hold on to them if we struck turbulence. I then noticed that there were signs on the walls of the fuselage to the effect that 'writing on the walls was not permitted' — No graffiti! The flight across the mountains to Aden's Khormakshar airport was considerably bumpy, but otherwise uneventful.

On arrival I was met by a second secretary from the embassy and his wife and, after formalities, we drove to the Rock Hotel, which I remembered from previous visits to Aden before and after the war. Driving through the town I was struck by the general air of decrepitude, empty streets, old British barracks occupied by Arab families living in congested accommodation, and a harbour devoid of any shipping. This, then, was the Marxist–Leninist 'paradise' of the People's Democratic Republic. I was forewarned that my room was 'bugged', but as I was unlikely to entertain there this gave me no concern. The hotel in which I was the only British guest appeared to be patronized largely by Russians, East Germans, Chinese communists and a handful of Italians. However, the accommodation was of a reasonable standard, the bar seemed to be permanently open and there was a restaurant/night-club on the roof garden — so I settled down to enjoy Aden during my enforced stopover there.

That evening I joined the second secretary and his wife for dinner at a restaurant on the roundabout to Khormakshar airport, which had excellent French food and wine, presumably smuggled in from Djibouti. I spent the next morning exploring the deserted streets and erstwhile duty-free shops (selling out-of-date radios and other goods) at Steamer Point, and paid a rewarding visit to the museum, established during the British occupation, where I and two Chinese were the only visitors. The museum was immaculately maintained and packed with Himarytic/Sabean artefacts, presumably looted and imported from Marib in North Yemen.

Our ambassador had invited me to accompany him for a swim that afternoon on one of the more remote beaches (with no shark-proof netting), which I had accepted with pleasure. While I was waiting to be picked up from the hotel lobby, a party of Russians arrived and complained vociferously to the reception clerk that they had been cheated by their taxi driver. The head porter, who was seated on an upturned soap box by the door, expressed his disapproval of the Russians' conduct by gesturing to me that they had big mouths; he then gave them a two-finger 'up yours' — British culture had survived!

I entertained my friends from the embassy to dinner that evening at our restaurant/nightclub and was surprised to see a notice over the entrance forbidding 'dancing without a lady'. The six-piece band was comprised of Somalis serving prison sentences at Khormakshar gaol who had been released for the evening on parole. On the third day, I claimed my return ticket via Beirut to London from my MEA friend Ibrahim and left Aden with no regrets — there was still no shipping in the harbour. Thus ended my mission to the Yemen, though I had not counted on being stranded and then diverted via Aden on the way home.

In due course, we recruited a retired senior police officer with experience in central Africa and the Gulf. He manfully endeavoured to establish a CID in the Yemen Arab Republic, but was thwarted in his attempt to set up a fingerprint bureau because so many convicted criminals had had their fingers chopped off for previous offences. He left after witnessing a crucifixion of a political dissident in the square outside his office — so much for the twentieth century in the Yemen.

Guyana revisited
During my 14 years' tenure of office (1966–79) in the Foreign and Commonwealth Office as Overseas Police Adviser/Inspector-General of Police, Dependent Territories, I visited Guyana twice, first in 1966 and then in 1978.

The first visit was of a stereotyped formal nature, with calls on the deputy prime minister, the minister of home affairs, the commander of the defence force, the US and Canadian aid agencies (on police training programmes) and all police departments. It also coincided with the annual reception of the Guyana British Legion, where I met many old Second World War soldiers.

However, the second visit, exactly 12 years later in November 1978, was of a much more eventful nature. By then the police force, in deference to the lurch to leftist political philosophies by the prime minister, Forbes Burnham, had become the 'People's Police Force' and I was invariably referred to as 'Comrade Mike'. I stayed with Philip Mallet, the British high commissioner who had only been *en poste* for a couple of months, and I engaged myself in the usual round of visits to police establishments and the Guyana Defence Force headquarters. While at the latter, I was offered a flight in the GDF's Islander light aircraft into the interior up to the Rupununi Province on the Brazilian border. I accepted it with enthusiasm and Philip asked if he could accompany the party, which was readily agreed. Little did we know that we were in for a very adventurous and stressful 11-hour day. Our rendezvous was at Timeiri (formerly Atkinson) international airport, where we met our GDF pilot, Captain Perieira, an Amerindian by birth.

Our flight was to be over the dense Orinoco rainforest, then across the Demerara and Essiquibo rivers to the spectacular Kaietur Falls, and on to the Rupununi via Orinduik on the Brazilian border to Lethem, the main centre in the Rupununi. However, after half an hour Captain Perieira informed us that there was 'a small problem' and we would have to make an emergency landing at Bartica, close to the notorious 'Jonestown' cult settlement. Having landed safely at Bartica, the pilot walked along the starboard wing and then, without further comment, we took off to return to Timeiri airport from where we had started.

The return flight lasted only 20 minutes, flying at 500 feet. On landing, we taxied to a hangar whereupon, on inspection, we were told that we had taken off originally before the starboard wing fuel-tank cap had been secured — thus losing approximately 20 gallons of aviation spirit in mid-flight. Before takeoff for the second time, we were informed that the ground staff would be 'disciplined' for this omission, though I learned later that no further action had been taken.

We then set course westwards for the Kaietur Falls, a spectacular cataract in the heart of the Amazonian forest. There was an airstrip above the falls, so we disembarked and walked through the forest to their edge. We were the only people there, so had an uninterrupted private view and a number of memorable photographs were taken for the record. After this very pleasant diversion, we flew to Orinduik on the Brazilian border, where a unit of the Guyana Defence Force and two policemen were stationed. We learned that, because of its remoteness, it had not been visited by inspecting officers from Georgetown in the previous six months. There were no recreational facilities there, no transistor radio or any books, and the staff had to borrow money from the assistant commissioner of police who was acting as our guide and escort.

From there we flew to Lethem, the main settlement in the Rupununi Province where, in 1970, there had been an uprising among the ranchers in which bazookas and automatic weapons were used and seven police officers were killed. The bullet and shell marks were still visible on the walls of the police station. All the rebels had escaped across the Brazilian border, so the Guyana Defence Force burnt down the local hotel and settlers' club in retaliation. While at the police station I wished to relieve myself and was conducted to a 'thunderbox' in the compound, to which I was somewhat surprised to find a bull tethered. When I asked whether this was an unavoidable hazard, I was blandly informed that it was a 'security measure' against intruders.

The final leg of this 11-hour flight into the interior involved a visit to the brand-new Linden highway, which — devoid of traffic but equipped with toll gates and speed control checks — appeared to lead from nowhere to nowhere. We were very relieved thereafter to land safely but exhausted at Timeiri international airport, only to be informed that we were to attend an evening reception given by the commissioner of police in honour of his travel-worn guests.

Up the Khyber — and the Hindu Kush (1973)
Early in May 1973 I embarked on a 23-day tour of south Asia

with three formidable assignments; the first to Pakistan, at the request of the director of the intelligence bureau (DIB) who had overall jurisdiction of the country's internal security apparatus, including the police force, to discuss training requirements in Britain; the second to Sri Lanka (which I had visited previously during the period of insurgency in 1971); and finally to Afghanistan, in the company of a Foreign Office colleague, to assess the viability of an aid project to establish an HF command radio network for the Afghan gendarmerie, as well as external training requirements.

The tour of Pakistan commenced in Karachi, where I was met by Colonel Mahmoud Majeed Quereshi of the DIB; he was based in Rawalpindi and acted as my escort throughout. We then flew to Rawalpindi, from where we continued by road to Islamabad, where I stayed with the British acting high commissioner, Reg Hobden and his wife Gwen, who were old friends from East African service days. As it was the weekend, we spent the Saturday night in the high commissioners bungalow 'Wild Rose', 7000 feet up in the Karakoram foothills, with stunning scenery and views, trees and birds to watch. I awoke on the Sunday morning to the call of the cuckoo. It was then back to Islamabad and Rawalpindi the same morning, a call at DIB headquarters and then off by air to Peshawar, the North-West Frontier headquarters, that evening, to be met by the regional inspector-general of police and accommodated in a cottage in the grounds of Dean's Hotel where, to my embarrassment, a quarter guard of the police had been posted. As Pakistan was officially 'dry', I was obliged later in the evening to entertain my hosts, the inspector-general of police and his staff officer, in my cottage to generous tots of Scotch from my duty-free ration with which I invariably travelled.

The following day was memorable. Commencing with a drive up the Khyber Pass, under armed escort because of our proximity to so-called tribal territory, we passed rocks containing the commemoration plaques of British Indian Army regiments that had served in the Khyber area in the past, all in immaculate condition and not vandalized by graffiti. We then stopped at Landikotal, the headquarters of the Khyber Rifles, where an officer of the Khyber Rifles was assigned to conduct me around three observation posts on the Afghan border. From there we could overlook illegal caravan routes in the tribal areas, along which smugglers were moving contraband merchandise (hardware, lorry tares and so forth, mostly from Russia through Afghanistan) by camel, by-passing the main road (under central government control) to the market they used in Landikotal. *En route*, we overtook a 'taxi' (a clapped-out Cadillac) with no less than 28 fare-paying passengers on board and aloft. After paying a short visit to the Landikotal bazaar, in which most of the wares for sale had been smuggled into Pakistan (I contented myself with the purchase of a communist Chinese toothbrush), we headed back to the Khyber Rifles officers' mess in the cantonment, where I lunched as the guest of the commanding officer, Colonel Mughal, and enjoyed the decorum and traditions of the Raj.

On our return down the pass we had to stop to allow a train to steam its way up. Once back in Peshawar, after a visit to the Kishakhamis bazaar, I spent an hour in the Gandara museum and then prepared myself for a dinner given by the North-West Frontier's inspector-general of police and local garrison commander at the officers' mess, where we were plied with Scotch whisky and entertained by Katak dancers from the tribal areas of the frontier — it was a truly memorable occasion.

The next port of call was Lahore, capital of the Punjab Province, to which, accompanied by Colonel Majeed Quereshi, I flew the next morning and checked in at Faletti's Hotel, a well-known meeting place in the days of the Raj and distinguished by its air of faded Victorian comfort. After a number of official calls and a private meeting with an old retired police superintendent from Tanganyika days, now comfortably and profitably established in a major French motor agency, we visited the 300-year-old Badshai Mosque, which can accommodate 100,0000 worshippers, and the Mogul fort. In the evening I attended the inspector-general of police's dinner at the police officers' mess, after which I was invited to 'conduct' the police band to the strains of 'Colonel Bogey'. On our return to Faletti's, Colonel Quereshi suggested we had a nightcap in the hotel nightclub, where we were surprisingly entertained by a middle-aged Pakistani lady 'stripper', presumably for the delectation of decadent foreign guests.

The itinerary was continued the following day with an approximately two and a half hour flight to Quetta, the provincial capital of Baluchistan, during which we caught a view of the *Mooltan* from the air. I was accommodated in the Circuit House, the government guesthouse, formerly in the days of the Raj reserved for circuit judges, and lunched shortly after arrival with the inspector-general of police, Baluchistan Province. He proved to be a charming and intellectual host, a historian and a member of the Central Asian Society. After an afternoon spent in his head-quarters, I dined that evening at the Police Club, an ex-regimental mess where all the formalities of a mess night were observed, except that the minstrel's gallery was not in use. Nevertheless, the general atmosphere was such that one felt the presence of the ghosts of the Indian Army in the days of the Raj.

The programme the next day was curtailed by a roaring dust storm; it reduced visibility to 50 yards and persisted into the after-noon, thereby delaying my onward flight to Karachi by three hours. We filled in the time with an uncomfortable visit to the bazaar. Before leaving, the group of police and army officers accompanying me jocularly suggested that if I was further delayed they would escort me to the mountains, where I could spend the night with a tribal chieftain whose hospitality would extend to providing one of his daughters to keep me warm. Fortunately, I escaped this experience by boarding a late flight to Karachi.

My final billet in Pakistan was in a palatial house in the shel-tered suburb of Clifton, south of the city, as a guest of Peter McEntee and his wife. They were old friends from colonial days in East Africa where Peter had been in the Kenya provincial adminis-tration. On the first evening, after supper with my host at the Talk of the Town restaurant, I was escorted by the inspector-general of police, Sind Province, of which Karachi is the capital, to the Oasis nightclub. The floor show, which was unique, was performed by Pakistani teenage girls specializing in traditional dances, closely watched by their mothers who ensured that they were whisked away immediately after the show. The next two days were spent at meetings with the DIB officer in Karachi and with the police, broken by a motor-patrol boat tour of the harbour, a long walk along the Sandspit beach and cocktail parties and suppers, culmin-ating in the inspector-general's banquet at the Intercontinental

Hotel. My first and only official visit to Pakistan can best be described as memorable.

The second leg of this long and demanding tour was by air to Sri Lanka, which I had visited on a previous occasion in 1971, when, at 24 hours' notice, I was dispatched in company with a brigadier from the Ministry of Defence to advise the Sri Lankan army and police force on measures to counter the widespread insurgency which had broken out in the island. On this occasion, normality having been restored, the tempo was more orderly. I was accommodated in the senior police officers' mess and, over a period of four days, carried out a full programme of visits to police establishments, including the training school at Kalutara. Because my visit coincided with the Republic Day parades, the inspector-general of police, Stanley Senanayake, arranged through the chief of protocol for a seat to be reserved for me in the presidential stand, where Mrs Bandaranaike took the salute as literally thousands of troops, police and youth organizations marched past during the two-hour parade. It was a historic bonus.

Somehow, I was next due to travel to Kabul, Afghanistan, from Colombo. This involved endless delays, both on leaving Sri Lanka and *en route* to Kahope, in the Punjab, where I was to connect with an Afghan Air flight. Fortunately, the British consul general in Lahore provided me with overnight accommodation and I eventually made the connection at Lahore airport, only to discover on boarding the Afghan Air flight that, because of strained relations between Pakistan and Afghanistan, the airport services had refused to clear the inboard toilets. Consequently, when we were airborne for Kabul, there was considerable seepage through the bulkheads into the passenger cabin. However, we arrived safely at Kabul airport and, somewhat the worse for wear, I was whisked off by an embassy car to the Intercontinental Hotel. The six days in Afghanistan proved to be an unforgettable experience.

After contacting my FCO colleague from London, who joined me for the visit, we called on the British ambassador, Mr John Drinkall (a former Indian Army officer), at the elegant Victorian residence in the embassy compound and attended a number of meetings with his staff, being joined later by the American Drug Enforcement Administration officer and members of the West

German police training team who had ongoing projects in Afghanistan, to reconcile our aid projects. Lunch at the embassy was followed by a courtesy call on the Afghan minister of the interior. After an evening cocktail party and supper at the embassy, we retreated to the Intercontinental Hotel, which was on a commanding hillside site overlooking the city, for the night.

It must be emphasized that this was early in 1973 when many problems faced the Afghan government, including political instability, a proliferation in the drug traffic and thousands of Western hippies and backpackers on the Kathmandu trail. For example, the US drug enforcement officer uncovered a clandestine container-borne traffic in drugs using his routes through Soviet Russia to the Black Sea. The West Germans were involved in modernizing the CID and traffic control branches of the gendarmerie and, as stated at the beginning of this chapter, we were doing a feasibility study on providing an HF command network for all the main provincial control centres. In addition, the embassy had one second secretary assigned principally to the welfare of convicted drug-running British backpackers and, because of appalling prison conditions, burying the dead, mostly victims of hepatitis or dysentery contracted during their enforced confinement. While in Kabul, I learned that the dead body of a teenage American girl drug addict had been found in a storm-weather drain in the city and that the bodies of a hitch-hiking young British couple had just been discovered in the desert on the main road near Kandahar, several months after they had been reported missing. On my return to Britain, I had the unenviable task of contacting their parents to inform them of their children's fate.

My programme included a meeting with the commandant general of the gendarmerie and visits to the transport, traffic, telecommunication, mounted and *Kriminalamt* (CID) branches of the gendarmerie. On the second day there were further meetings with Dr Mansouri, the special adviser to the prime minister, and other senior government officials, followed by a welcome break with General Abdul Ghani, the commandant general to the Kabul Gorge, along the Salalabad road to Paghman (the royal palace), Kharga Lake and the Tangi Gharq.

Given that the last working day was a Friday, we decided to

take a drive (in a Volkswagen Jeep thanks to German aid) up the Salang Pass via Qara Bagh, Charikaa and the Jebel Seraj, through the Hindu Kush (up to 11,000 feet high) on the Russian-built road and tunnel to Khimjan on the north side, where we lunched at the Khimjan Hotel, patronized almost exclusively by Russians and their families, before retracing our route through the Hindu Kush to Kabul. *En route*, we had no less than five breakdowns and were eventually 'rescued' by a German driving a Mercedes. He turned out to be the regional representative of the Volkswagen Group, so I invited him that evening to drinks at the Intercontinental so that he could explain the shortcomings of the Volkswagen Jeeps to a selected group of senior Afghan police officers.

Before leaving Kabul, I managed to fit in a short visit to the bazaar and purchased an elegant Afghan carpet — machine-made in Herat on the Iranian border — which I carried back to Heathrow, much to the surprise of the customs officers, who exempted me from paying duty.

On the morning of my departure, General Abdul Ghani,[1] my host for the week, came into the departure lounge to bid me farewell. He kissed me on both cheeks and said, 'Good night my dear', much to the amusement of a young American woman who, unfortunately, was sitting next to me on the aircraft and laughed all the way to Tehran. All in all, this had been an unexpectedly adventurous and bizarre assignment, but the coup put paid to implementation of the HF command network project — a saving for the British taxpayer?

In conclusion, I have to admit that I was often lucky enough during my long career to be selected to be in the Wrong Place at the Right Time. As Edith Piaf, the French chanteuse once sang, '*Non, je ne regrette rien.*'

---

1. I learned afterwards that General Ghani was a victim of the communist coup some months later and was last seen in a cage in the Kabul zoo.

Appendix A
German Political Organizations in Tanganyika, 1925–39[1]

German reinfiltration into what was the former colony of German East Africa followed swiftly on the lapse of the Ex-Enemies Restrictions Ordinance in June 1925. By the end of September the following year, 420 German families had already arrived in the territory. Some of these postwar pioneers bought up land in their own title and many were engaged by European and Asian landowners as plantation managers or servants. Others entered the territory as missionaries, prospectors, labour recruiters, road contractors, storekeepers, transport drivers and mangrove bark traders, to name a few of the many occupations adopted by this new flood of colonists.

A policy of peaceful penetration was steadily pursued and, in its furtherance, even the lowliest forms of employment were accepted by the new German colonists. Often the offer of a mere pittance was sufficient inducement for a German to engage himself in a position of servility to an Asian. One particularly striking instance was that of a former private secretary to a German colonial governor who in 1926 was working for an Indian at a wage of £20 a month.

A notable characteristic of these early settlers was their invariable ability to pay their immigration deposit in cash, ranging from

---

1. Culled from Special Branch research and records of 1939.

£50 for a single immigrant to £150 for a family exceeding three persons. Thus, it was reasonable to believe, in the circumstances, that behind this influx, some organization existed in Germany to provide approved immigrants with the necessary financial backing. And agents of this organization were soon at work in the territory. Among these was a prominent Silesian nobleman, Prince Gustav von Schoenauth Carolath, who was in direct communication with the famous postwar banker, Hugo Stinnes, and enjoyed considerable respect from the newly settled German community. Carolath also visited Portuguese East Africa, where German activities in Beira had increased and where considerable capital was being invested in the purchase of properties and the construction of houses. Two or three hundred German settlers were expected in this area.

As early as 1926 a Greek-owned, German-managed commercial concern with a registered capital of only £6000, the Usagara Company, was suspected of being the medium through which payments in Tanganyika were negotiated at the instance of the home organization. A director of the company admitted in conversation, however, that in four months no less than £250,000 was paid out.

Offers of enormous sums were made for coffee estates — in one instance £100,000 was bid for a valuable farm and, in another, £8000 for a small estate which, three years previously, had been bought for only £375. The chief centres of attraction for these early German colonists were the coffee producing districts of Arusha and Moshi, and the sisal belt traversed by the Tanga–Voi railway line. British opinion on this influx was best summarized in the words of the landowners who indifferently stated, 'If the Germans pay handsomely enough, let them have the land.'

Another aspect of German infiltration into the territory is contained in the actions of certain Indians who were prominent in their purchases at the sales of ex-enemy plantations. In several instances, it was suspected that properties were bought and secretly held for Germans who, at that time, were prohibited from purchasing. In fact, many Germans who appeared as managers of Indian plantations were probably *de facto* owners. Most notable among these Indian property owners was the wealthy firm of Karimjee Jivanjee, which showed a willingness to assist the new

German settlers and, in many indirect ways, subsidized German enterprise.

The general attitude of the returning German colonists was one of outward conciliation. They were obsequious towards officials, friendly with the Asians and benign to the Africans. By stifling their inherent bombast and pride they played a difficult part, striving to create a favourable impression and to establish themselves as an acceptable people.

On the other side, the British settler community started to show a natural feeling of uneasiness as regards the ultimate destiny of the territory and, with the return of the German settlers, the fear that it would be restored to Germany was more and more frequently expressed. Thus, in 1926 there were many who already forecasted a restoration to Germany of her former East African colony.

In Germany, the ex-colonists were agitating for the formation of a Chartered Company for African Colonial Development. Dr Schacht of the Reichsbank and von Schubert of the German Foreign Office gave their full support and British capital assistance was eagerly courted. Germany was aiming to regain pre-eminence in her former colonies through peaceful commercial penetration. The Westafrikanische Pflanzungsgesellschaft 'Victoria' was set up with the following board of directors: Udo Prinz zu Loewenstein (Wetheim-Freudenberg); Cal Hagen and Louis Hagen (bankers); Georg Seitz (treasury official); Dr Albert Ahn (economic expert); and Rudolf Seitz, Hugo Scholler, R. F. Wahl and Wilhelm Kenner (lawyers) — the campaign had started.

By 1932 the German government had ceased to pretend it had no designs for the reannexation of its former East African colony. Settlers were arriving in scores at the ports of Dar es Salaam and Tanga. They were met by agents of the Usagara Company, now definitely associated with the German government, who welcomed them, paid their immigration deposits, shepherded them through customs and saw them safely onto trains leaving for the highlands of the interior. Many of these settlers arrived with large numbers of firearms, which they often explained away by stating that they had been told before leaving the fatherland that arms were indispensable for use against the natives who had become very truculent under British rule.[2] Prospective German settlers were also encouraged to wear jackboots as protection against snakebite.

A German Association already existed with the definite aim of increasing German representation and influence in the affairs of the territory. Simultaneously, a noticeable increase of pro-German propaganda was evident among native communities throughout the territory. There were many cases of insubordination by natives against Europeans, and a native's invariable reply on being taken to task on his attitude was that he had been told that the Germans were returning, and with them prosperity and work for all.

With the advent of Hitler in 1933 many Germans who had formerly hidden their sympathies under a cloak of discretion came out into the open and Nazi meetings with much flag-waving and speech-making were held in various parts of the territory.

Admiral Menche of the German navy visited Tanga, and a meeting of 200 Nazis was held in his honour at which Nazi uniforms were worn. Germans went out of their way to 'assert' themselves; there were incidents of public flaunting of the swastika; of Union Jacks being torn from British settlers' cars; and of native assaults on British-employed *askari*s. An ex-German colonial secretary toured the territory and a German Association for East Africa was formed. Whenever a German vessel arrived in a Tanganyikan port, a political meeting invariably took place; swastika flags began to appear at native *ngoma*s (dances); ex-German *askari*s were influenced or bribed into a fanatical belief in the inevitable return of their former masters, and cases of terrorization by these same ex-soldiers were not unknown.

During this period reports came in from various parts of the territory to the effect that local Germans were drilling and practising military exercises. Some members of the crew of a German vessel in Tanga harbour were caught rehearsing a landing from an open boat, and photographs seized at the outbreak of war show Northern Province Germans on route marches, field exercises and practising grenade-throwing. The great Nazi weapon of propa-

---

2. The terminology used and sentiments expressed in this Appendix reflect those in current use in official British documents and reports in the period during the build-up to the Second World War.

ganda was adeptly used — with a flood of pamphlets and books finding their way into the territory. Attempts were made to popularize the regime through special cinema performances and social gatherings with consistently pro-Nazi undertones. Many natives employed on German plantations gave the Nazi salute and definite proof was obtained that in certain cases this was done at the direct instigation of German plantation owners.

Up until the autumn of 1922 there had been very little concrete evidence of the existence of the Nazi Party in the territory, its activities for some time being confused with those of the German Association. However, an auspicious burglary at the office of the treasurer of the Moshi branch of the party provided an opportunity to scrutinize party papers. It was found that emoluments were distributed liberally from October 1933 onwards. Among the signed party declaration forms of new members, were found those of many of the prominent Germans of the district, some of whom later held office in the party. The declaration form was identical to the one the Nazi Party in Germany used to enrol new members.

The pioneer German Association, the Deutscher Bund, was inaugurated at a meeting of representative Germans from all parts of the territory in July 1933 at Dodoma, Central Province, and in a semi-official capacity it directed German affairs until the end of 1934. The Nazis then began to come out into the open and Troost, manager of the Usagara Company's training school at Altona, near Hamburg, was announced as *Landesgruppenleiter* for the whole territory, as well as *Ortsgruppenleiter* for the Moshi District.

In December 1934, Troost and Captain von Schoenfeld, leader of the Deutscher Bund, had a violent quarrel in Moshi over the respective standing of their organizations, Troost contending that as leader of the Nazi Party in Tanganyika he was the direct representative of Herr Hitler and the German government. He insisted that the Deutscher Bund was under the direct and absolute control of the NSDAP and he therefore demanded obedience from its members. There were two very stormy meetings at Moshi, at one of which Herr Troost is reported to have administered the Nazi vow to many Germans present and to have stated that 'all orders given by the leader in Germany to his representative in East Africa

119

must be obeyed even to the extent of going against the "Mandate" government.' The outcome of this dispute was the resignation of Captain von Schoenfeld from the leadership of the Deutscher Bund and the election of Dr I. P. Zitzlaff, a settler from Usa River, Arusha in his stead.

There can be little doubt that, since the beginning of 1935, the only political power among the Germans in the territory was the NSDAP, which made every attempt to relegate the Bund to a secondary position within the party and subject it to the dictates of Troost. Troost had the backing of the younger element, many of the older Germans viewing his activities with disfavour, although some of the latter became members of the party for convenience. Reports were frequently received that German settlers joined the party solely because they feared reprisals for failing to do so. In Tanga, where most of the Germans were members of the party, the party itself was not popular and its officials were persons of little social or commercial importance.

Correspondence between a prominent local German and the director of the foreign service in Berlin, Lieutenant-Colonel Kuentzel, written during 1934/5 and seized and examined at the outbreak of war, revealed the following salient points concerning Nazi organization in Tanganyika:

> It is the generally acknowledged duty of every government to be informed of the position and development of other governments. Also, there is a German principle which states that every friend of the Fatherland who lives aboard has the right and duty to notify those at home of all important matters that he may see or hear. The most valuable information is that obtained through professional channels. . . .
>
> Reports from abroad are considered to be so important that they are now being passed on to the deputy of the Führer (Herr Hess) for his consideration. In this connection, it must be remembered that such matters as labour conditions, economics, commercial relations, export and import conditions (especially textiles) are of most importance to the Fatherland. . . .
>
> So far as the German community in East Africa is con-

cerned, their main duties come under the following head-ings:

1. Expansion and development of Nazi ideals — through the NSDAP.
2. Supervision of morals and business methods — through the party and the Deutscher Bund.
3. Disputes and arbitration: between party members through the NSDAP, otherwise through the Deutscher Bund.
4. Advice on legal, health and other questions — by the Deutscher Bund in cooperation with the Bund Deutscher Frauen (German Women's League).
5. General legal assistance — through the Deutscher Bund.
6. Grants-in-aid — through the party, Deutscher Bund and Frauenbund.
7. Commercial and trade questions, economic cooperation, financial advice, distribution of labour, etc. — through the party and the Deutscher Bund.
8. Cultural Matters: (a) Religious matters — through the Deutscher Bund; (b) literature and newspapers — through the party, Deutscher Bund and Frauenbund; (c) educational matters — the party and the Deutscher Bund.
9. Representation of German interests: internal questions (political).
10. Representation of the German community at public celebrations, visits, etc. — through the party or the Deutscher Bund.[3]

---

3. This division was agreed to by the central authorities on 4 January 1935 but met with instant opposition from the various foreign *Landesgruppenleiter*s (regional leaders). It was evident from the start in East Africa that there would be a split between the party and the Deutscher Bund owing to duplication of functions and internal jealousy. On the other hand, certain party members in the Southern Province wished to retain the Deutscher Bund, as it would provide an alternative organization if the Tanganyika government followed the action of the South African government in banning the Nazi Party in the territory as had been done in South West Africa.

So far as East Africa is concerned it is the duty of all party officials to obtain as much information as possible on native unrest and communist propaganda in the territories. In this respect, any hint of closer union too must be reported forthwith to the central office in Berlin. Any local difficulties should be referred to the German consulate, Nairobi. The objects of our organization should be kept in view; reports on movements of aircraft and technical development would be particularly welcome.[4]

On instructions from Berlin it was decided to preserve the Deutscher Bund in its present form, political leaders of the Bund acting as private individuals and not as members of the Nazi Party. Evidence in correspondence shows that the Deutscher Bund was still in operation in Tanganyika Territory as late as 1938.

One of the most important branches of the party's activities was the Hitler Youth Movement, which was inaugurated in the territory in February 1934. In less than six months it had recruited so many young Nazis that it had fallen into disfavour with the older and more moderate Germans who feared that its zeal might result in the withdrawal of the government subsidy from their schools. Little was then heard of the movement until the beginning of 1936, when rumours of the formation of training camps for young Germans was received. A new sports club, with dormitories and messing accommodation, was built in Dabaga and it was suggested that this was to be used as one of the camps. The organization of the Hitler Youth continued to exercise considerable influence over German youths in the territory up to the outbreak of war. Conscription had been applied to all young Germans in the territory who were leaving in batches for military training in Germany, to return subsequently with a working knowledge of modern war methods.

---

4. This close liaison between the Berlin directive and the party's representatives throughout the world was maintained even to the extent of information of mislaid mails and their countries of origin being passed back to all foreign branches of the NSDAP and Deutscher Bund.

Nazi women in the territory were organized politically through the association, Bund Deutscher Frauen.

German Labour Front (Deutsche Arbeitsfront)
The following summary on the organization of the German Labour Front in Tanganyika is based on extracts from correspondence seized from the territorial organization on the outbreak of war. The greater part of the thousands of letters examined contained unimportant material on accounts, transfers, promotions and propaganda, but at the same time they gave an accurate picture of the history of the organization and its functions within the territory.

The organization had its origins in the German National Commercial Assistants' Union (*Deutscher Nationale Handlungsgehilfenverband* — DNHV). Correspondence from this body was received in Tanganyika as early as 1931. At that time, it was a union protecting the interests of commercial clerks and employees. It had no political significance. In the two years prior to the advent of Nazi rule in Germany the DNHV gradually came under the wing of the *Deutsche Nationalpartei* (German National Party) — the royalist organization.

In 1933 the name of the union was changed to the *Deutscher Handlungsgehilfenverband* (German Commercial Assistants' Union) and the connection with the royalist party was severed. The territorial headquarters of the reorganized union was at Tanga and had the following officials:

Otto Hinrichs	*Stützpunktleiter* (help-post warden) previously Tanganyika representative of the DNHV
Bruno Wilrich	Secretary
J. F. W. Schulze	Treasurer
E. Riediger	Propaganda warden

The first local *Stützpunkt* was established at Dodoma (Brodersen). This was followed by the creation of others at Moshi (Bernhard Moeller), Dar es Salaam (Limmer) and elsewhere.

It is unclear what the initial aims of the organization were, but from correspondence it is evident that it was primarily occupied with questions of economics, commerce, exports and professional training after the model of German commercial training schools.

The whole organization became a part of the greater body, the German Labour Front. The various bodies controlled by the Labour Front were urged to cooperate, especially abroad. Evidence of this was obtained from references in circular letters from the DHV headquarters in Hamburg advocating closer cooperation with such bodies as the German Fichte Bund (propaganda press).

The DHV and other subsidiary unions enjoyed a very short life under the Nazi regime, for they were all incorporated in a new and wider organization known as the German Employees' Union (*Deutsche Angestelltenschaft*). There was as yet no suggestion of open fusion with the German political organizations abroad, but non-commercial matters appeared in all correspondence and politics and propaganda came to the fore in the subject matter of letters.

Pressure was increased so as to recruit all Germans for the Labour Front, anti-Jewish laws were introduced, and intimidation through boycott of sales and threats of reprisals in Germany became customary. The organization was extended; cells (*Stützpunkte*) and town groups were established on the recommendation of the Nazi leaders, and nearly all official posts were filled by members of the Nazi Party. By the beginning of 1935 the organization changed its name for the third time and became the Foreign Office of German Professional Groups (*Auslandsamt der Deutschen Berufsgruppen*). In this connection, it is interesting to note that E. W. Bohle, the *Gauleiter* of the foreign organization of the Nazi Party, referred in a letter to India in 1937 to the foreign trade office of the *Auslandsorganisation* (apparently the *Auslandsamt der Deutschen Berufsgruppen*, which was recognized by the German Foreign Office as the only representative body for the interests of Germans abroad, and which had its offices at Hochhaus am Holsteinwall, Hamburg 36) as the greatest achievement of the whole system. (Ref. Government of India Political Intelligence Survey No. 25 of 1939, for the week ending 4 November 1939.)

At the same time the relationship between this representative branch of the German Labour Front and the Nazi Party was openly admitted. Each group was instructed to nominate its officials — the warden, treasurer, secretary, propaganda-warden, 'Strength through Joy' (spare-time organization) warden, labour exchange warden, and so forth.

All Nazi Party members in the area were to be encouraged to join the Labour Front. The argument used was that it was the will of the Führer that every German Nazi must also be a member of the only professional organization in Germany. It was decided subsequently that only members of the Nazi Party could hold office in the Labour Front, but that membership of the latter would be reckoned as a qualification for membership of the Nazi Party itself.

Political propaganda was disseminated by means of circulars, periodicals, pamphlets and films in ever-increasing quantities. By unceasing efforts, small German communities were formed all over the world. From one list published in a circular of 16 December 1933, places as far apart as Buffalo (USA) and Sourabaya (Java) or Luxembourg and Lima (Peru) boasted of Nazi *Stützpunkte*. As soon as a cell had eight subscribing members it was promoted to a *Stützpunkte* (help-post). The officials were duly promoted and a rubber stamp was issued inscribed 'German Labour Front, Overseas Organization, *Stützpunkt*'. The event was ceremoniously carried out and important-looking documents were sent from Germany. If the *Stützpunkt* succeeded in recruiting 30 members it was duly raised to the status of town group (*Ortsgruppe*). The promotion would be confirmed in due course from Berlin and a suitably inscribed group flag would be forwarded as part of the regalia.

In Tanganyika, the various subdivisions were under the control of the *Landesgruppe*. In 1938 the *Landesgruppe* was divided into two main groups — north and south — each with its local leader. The whole of the organization was under the control of Paul Fuchs, a sub-manager of the Usagara Company, Dar es Salaam. This young man of 26 described himself as 'Nazi No. 2 of Tanganyika'.

The officials of the groups were frequently changed owing to transfers, leave or inefficiency. Throughout the correspondence to all officials there is constant repetition of the importance of their work. Letters were written in military form and were orders rather than requests. Junior officials were permitted to correspond direct with Berlin and thus acquired a sense of importance and official superiority.

Most of the Germans in Tanganyika were members, for there were covert threats that membership would be useful, especially when on leave in Germany. In the last year or two much was made of the probable return of Tanganyika to the Reich 'in a few weeks'. All local officials, on going home on leave, were provided with a letter of introduction to the foreign organization office of the Labour Front and were obliged to call there. They were also expected to undergo a training course at one of the political schools. Gifts, generally books, were sent from Germany to the *Landesgruppe* for presentation to the most efficient officials.

On the financial side, the Nazi officials' most important function was the collection of funds. Members' subscriptions were based on their income or salary, which they had to declare. These were collected by the treasurer of the nearest group. Members whose subscriptions were more than three months in arrears were liable to expulsion from the party. This rule was very rarely enforced. After deduction of a small percentage for local working expenses, the subscriptions were sent through the Usagara Company to the treasurer at Tanga, who then transferred the amount to Berlin. Small grants were made from the local funds to the unemployed, sick and other distressed persons. All official positions were honorary, but travelling expenses were met in part.

The German Labour Front had a particular interest in the maintenance of the good reputation of Germans within the territory, and urged that differences should be settled. Admiral Forster von Bohlen, the chief of the German East Africa Line (DOAL), took the opportunity to visit Tanganyika and attend local German patriotic meetings. At the same time, reports came through of German missionary participation in Nazi activities, and rumours that Tanganyika would be handed back to Germany as often as not emanated from native mission sources or from areas in which the only European would be a German Lutheran or Roman Catholic missionary. German agitation aggravated native coffee

126

riots in the Lake and Northern provinces and even female missionaries were seen conversing with demonstrators.

The mass of Germans in the territory were under some form of
political control or organization from the early days of reinfiltration and their influence was considerable throughout all spheres of
life and all communities in the territory. Their internal organization was disciplined and efficient and their attempts at preparing
native opinion for their return as masters of the territory were
painstakingly thorough.

The comparative ease in rounding up all males at the outbreak
of war and their total lack of resistance was based not so much on
their inability to resist as on the improbability of obtaining outside
assistance. If Italy had entered the war in September 1939 instead
of June 1940, the concluding stages of German political activities
in former German East Africa (1925–39) would undoubtedly have
read differently.

Appendix B
Prewar Nazi Penetration of East Africa and its Potential Threat, 1939–40

On the outbreak of war in September 1939 there were more Germans than British in the private sector in Tanganyika, particularly in the coffee, tea and sisal farming communities. The British mandate administration, among whom a number of senior officials were demonstrably pro-German (mainly as a result of their personal and social relationships with the German community), rather reluctantly decided to detain and intern all adult German males.

A small number evaded arrest by escaping to neutral Portuguese-administered Mozambique. The others, some 3000 in all, were rounded up by the Tanganyika administration and police and interned centrally in a converted public-works stores compound on the Pugu Road just outside the capital, Dar es Salaam. These internees, who were loosely guarded by police and special constables, enjoyed the privilege of visits from relatives and were exercised daily by being marched — under army (King's African Rifles) escort — through the streets of Dar es Salaam to the nearby beaches.

Naturally, they took advantage of this concession and the early mornings often resounded to the strains of the 'Horst Wessel Lied' (the Nazi anthem) as they marched to their recreation. There were few, if any, of the administration in Tanganyika at the time who had any experience of the pervasive ruthlessness of the Nazi movement, and they treated their 'captives' as unfortunate enemy aliens who had been stranded in East Africa by the tide of war.

My personal introduction to Tanganyika coincided with the early days of the war in September 1939, when, after a year's training with the Metropolitan Police in London, I was posted as a cadet assistant superintendent of police to Dar es Salaam. After a long sea journey via Suez (war was declared when we were in Port Said), punctuated by delays and blackouts (notably in Port Tewfik at the southern end of the canal where we lay at anchor offshore for a while), I arrived in Dar es Salaam to be posted forthwith to Special Branch in police headquarters.

Because I was a German speaker and before the war had been an *Auslandsstudent* on a German language and literature diploma course at a German university, I was marked out as a useful recruit to the embryonic security intelligence organization in Tanganyika. The director of intelligence and security, the energetic and forceful Scot named Neil Stewart, whom I succeeded in 1942, assigned me to the task of sifting the mass of documents seized from German internees, and of identifying the scale and significance of the Nazi penetration of the German community.

After several weeks of painstaking research, in which I was ably assisted by Eleanor Lewis, a senior secretary, and Roland Fodbey, a young half-Danish police inspector, both of whom were also fluent German speakers, a pattern of widespread and thorough organization, planning and subversion emerged.

It was clear from our research that, with the prospect of war between Germany and the Western Allies, a network of Nazi units and cells had been established in all the German communities in the territory. The Nazi Party lists and documents that came into our hands revealed a comprehensive organization with a *Landesgruppenleiter* (territorial leader), *Kreis* and *Gauleiter* (provincial and district leaders), as well as *Ortsgruppen* (district groups) throughout the country. Very few Germans (other than Jews) in the territory did not belong to the party, though there were a few older Germans (mostly ex-army officers) who professed to belong to the German National Party. This was a strongly conservative group which remained staunchly patriotic. Notable in this group

129

was a well-respected planter, Major Müller, who had been General von Lettow-Vorbeck's staff officer during the 1914–16 campaign in East Africa.

Müller was very popular with the British administration, for he typified an old-style German 'gentleman', and was left at liberty on parole on his plantation until the entry of Italy into the war in mid-1940. He subsequently escaped from internment in South Africa and spent the rest of the war in Mozambique.

Several borderline Nazis were likewise paroled. They were all 'gentlemen' and socially acceptable to the administration. However, on completion of our investigations towards the end of 1939, it was abundantly clear that we had detained all but a few of the hard-line Nazis, including all the leaders. The organization, as such, had been broken. The *Landesgruppenleiter*, Dr Ernst Troost, whom I interrogated on a number of occasions, was consistently uncooperative and aggressive. (He was eventually deported under armed escort and transported by British merchant vessel to an internment camp at Paignton Sands in Devon, where he was held for the duration.)

It might well be asked what the Nazis hoped to achieve in Tanganyika and to a lesser degree in Kenya and Uganda. However, as a result of our enquiries, it became evident that a contingency plan had been drawn up by the Nazi high command in the event of Italy's entry into the war in September 1939. The Nazis in Tanganyika were organized and trained to create diversionary actions in such an eventuality, on the assumption that there would be an Italian invasion of British East Africa. The groups in the Kilimanjaro and Tanga Province areas had orders to mount guerrilla tactics to disrupt the British lines of communication and were trained to this end.

A number of operational orders were discovered, as were photographs of Nazis drilling with weapons and training in field tactics in remote areas of northern Tanganyika. A major arms cache was alleged to have been established on the Shira plateau of western Kilimanjaro, but despite intensive searches it was never unearthed. In the meantime, due largely to the 'phoney war' and lack of hostilities in East Africa, a degree of tolerant complacency crept into the attitude of the government of Tanganyika towards its enemy aliens. Most of the wives and families of the German community were permitted to remain on their plantations 'on parole'. However, the German internees and their paroled families were by no means inactive. A systematic effort was made from the internment camp in Dar es Salaam, and by the paroled Germans still at large in the country, to subvert the many Africans who had family or service links with the former German administration during the First World War and afterwards. A number of ex-German *askaris*, including the editor of a local vernacular newspaper, Sykes Plantan, made no secret of their anti-British sentiments, which were supported and encouraged by their former masters. Some of the pro-German activists were 'rusticated' under an internal deportation ordinance and removed from the main centres of population.

By the beginning of 1940, the Tanganyika administration, presumably with the blessing of Whitehall, decided, largely on grounds of cost and the deployment of manpower, to repatriate all German males who could be classified as non-combatants. In the interim, the principal leaders of the Nazis in the camp had been segregated and placed in a camp on an island off the entrance to Dar es Salaam harbour known as Honeymoon Island. This had been very popular for weekend picnics, and the use of the island was generally resented by the residents of Dar es Salaam who felt they had been deprived of a recreational facility. The island camp was guarded by a small contingent of the King's African Rifles, but the hard-core internees were free to use the island and its beaches. They frequently appeared in the nude on the beaches, to the embarrassment and irritation of passing weekend yachtsmen! However, so lax was the security on the island that one night Troost, the *Landesgruppenleiter*, who was over 50 years of age, and Alex Herrgott, a young activist, swam ashore in an attempt to escape on foot to Mozambique. They were picked up by the police some 20 miles south of Dar es Salaam 48 hours later and committed to the cells.

In the meantime, arrangements had been made for the repatriation of those wives and children willing to return to Germany, as well as the so-called non-combatant males. The vetting of eligibility to join their category was so casual that many a 'non-combatant' was in the ranks of the *Wehrmacht* within weeks of returning to the Fatherland. Among those selected for repatriation was Herrgott, Troost's companion on the abortive escape attempt from Honeymoon Island. He appeared to be fully fit for active service. I joined a group of Tanganyika police officers to check on personal effects being taken by the repatriates. Several German women abused and spat at us during the search but, despite this, we were to be rewarded. When it came to Herrgott's turn, we searched a large tin box in which he had packed his personal effects. However, it was discovered that the box had a false bottom in which there was a *Luftwaffe* intelligence officer's uniform. Herrgott's bluff was blown and he was promptly arrested and returned to the cells. And we were subjected to further uncontrolled abuse. An interesting sequel to this discovery was the use of the uniform by the Long Range Desert Group of the Eighth Army in their raids behind Rommel's lines. Herrgott was eventually sent to South Africa and interned there for the duration.

Once the bulk of the German wives and families had been repatriated on Italian ships to Europe, we were left with those who were unwilling to leave their husbands, plus the majority of the males still in internment. With the entry of Italy into the war in June 1940, the Tanganyika government belatedly decided to deport all remaining Germans — male and female — to internment in South Africa and Rhodesia. The male internees were transported under heavy guard in troopships, and the women and children by passenger ships under a motley escort of police officers and women special constables, many of whom were secretariat wives. In most cases it was their only opportunity during the war to don a uniform.

Thus, by mid-1940, Tanganyika and the rest of East Africa (Kenya and Uganda took similar action with very much smaller numbers of enemy aliens) were free of the Nazi presence, the few remaining non-Nazi Germans having signed non-belligerent parole forms and remained free. Several of the latter joined the forces, having been declared stateless. As mentioned earlier (p.18), one in particular joined the Free French forces after having been refused enlistment into HM Forces, and gained a Croix de Guerre at Bir Hakeim in North Africa.

In conclusion, one might speculate what could have happened had Italy entered the war in September 1939. There is little doubt in the minds of those who had to deal with the incipient threat, so real in 1939, that the governments of the British East African territories would have been faced with the 'Fifth Column', particularly in Tanganyika, which would have been difficult if not impossible to contain.

Appendix C
The Todd Mission:
Madagascar, 1941–2

For many months prior to the Allied invasion of Vichy French-held Madagascar in May 1942, a British-manned clandestine reconnaissance and sabotage operation was active on the west coast of the island. Early on, it was decided to provide a backup base in Dar es Salaam, on the East African coast. My personal involvement, as director of intelligence and security in the Tanganyika police, covered the provision of a suitable craft, supplies and debriefing facilities. After a visit by Lieutenant-Commander Wilfred Hancock RN and Captain Alan Le Brocq, Royal Marines, of the Todd Mission, we charted a coastal schooner, the *Lindi*, which was owned by George Houry, a Greek Cypriot lawyer and businessman of Lebanese origin, who operated a number of small supply craft along the Tanganyikan coast.

Once Dar es Salaam had been established as a supply base, the *Lindi* paid visits in the ensuing month, including on one occasion when two British employees of the Bonamary meat factory near Majunga on the west coast of Madagascar were evacuated and handed over for debriefing and disposal. One of them, who had became very drunk while at the New Africa Hotel in Dar es Salaam, was irresponsibly indiscreet and had to be detained in police custody and removed to Nairobi *en route* to the Middle East.

134

During the same period (from the end of 1941 to early 1942) three incidents associated with Madagascar occurred. The first involved a French air force officer who commandeered a light aircraft in Diego Suarez and flew it to Lindi in southern Tanganyika. After interrogation he was sent on his way to join the Free French forces in the Middle East.

The second incident was highly unusual. One Sunday afternoon, a strange schooner sailed into Dar es Salaam harbour flying the Free French flag. On boarding the craft, we discovered that it had been stolen in Diego Suarez harbour by a motley group of Free French sympathizers and sailed the 700 miles direct to Dar es Salaam. The party on board consisted of a local bank manager, a doctor with his wife and 4-year-old daughter, five French army NCOs and a midwife. Their arrival created quite a stir — and a bonus for those planning the invasion of Madagascar, for the French army group brought with them detailed plans of the defences of Diego Suarez. After two weeks in Dar es Salaam, during which military experts from East Africa Command headquarters in Nairobi analysed the details of the plans and the midwife married the bank manager (with the district commissioner, Dar es Salaam, Andy Pike officiating and me as the sole witness), the party dispersed bound for the Middle East. I maintained contact with two of the French army NCOs, who subsequently fought in the ranks of the Free French forces in Syria, and survived the war.

The final chapter in this unusual association with the Madagascar campaign was enacted some weeks before the invasion when the British forces decided to stage a dress rehearsal of the Diego Suarez landings in Msasani Bay, just north of Dar es Salaam. Unfortunately, through an apparent lack of consultation and coordination, this coincided with the arrival of the first batch of 1200 Polish refugees from Russia who had travelled to East Africa via Tehran and Karachi. They were families and relatives of officers and men serving in the Allied forces with General Anders's Polish corps. As we were shepherding and processing large numbers of tired, frightened and lice-ridden Polish refugee women and children on their way to the transit camp outside Dar es Salaam, the train and camp were 'taken' by Royal Marines firing blank cartridges and giving every impression that the Poles had entered another battleground. Most of the refugees were terrified and we had considerable difficulty explaining the background to their very hostile reception on Tanganyikan soil.

From that day on, apart from scant newspaper reports, we were to hear little of further developments on the Madagascar front, other than the fact that resistance by the Vichy French forces and, in particular, by the Senegalese colonial troops, was much stiffer than anticipated by the planners of the invasion.

Appendix D
Episodes from Upcountry Tanganyika, 1945–7

The convicted murderer

This is a sad tale. On assuming charge of the police in the Southern Highlands Province of Tanganyika in 1946, I enquired from the staff at the headquarters in Mbeya if there were any outstanding cases of a serious nature awaiting completion of investigation or presentation to court.

Rather reluctantly, I was informed that there was indeed a major case involving a convicted murderer who had escaped without trace from the prison while awaiting execution some eighteen months previously. It was thought he might have escaped by crossing the interterritorial border either into Northern Rhodesia (Zambia) or Nyasaland (Malawi). I read the case file, which recorded a brutal *crime passionnel* in which the accused had speared his wife to death through the wall of their grass hut home while she was *in flagrante* with her lover. I asked what attempts, subsequent to the escape, had been made to circularize his particulars to the Northern Rhodesian and Nyasaland authorities. Apart from an initial telegram giving his name, tribe and brief description, which had been sent to Lusaka and Zomba, the matter had been allowed to rest.

I then redrafted a detailed 'wanted' notice and sent it not only to police headquarters in the neighbouring territories but also to Ndola in the Copperbelt, where a large number of alien labourers were employed on the mines. Within days a reply came to the effect that the wanted man had been employed at the Nchanga mine, but had left for his home in northern Nyasaland. It was then decided, with the full agreement of the Nyasaland authorities, to mount a discreet manhunt in his home district. I personally briefed an experienced Detective-Sergeant Levi, appropriately nicknamed 'Safari', and two young, active and intelligent constables, who were told not to mention their mission to anybody. They were given adequate subsistence, information and funds and, with an unlimited time scale, directed to cross the border into Nyasaland to try and trace the convicted murderer.

For some weeks there was no word from the team, but then I received a note from the sergeant to the effect that they were on his trail, that he knew this and was always one jump ahead of them. I told them to persevere. About two weeks later, while I was on a weekend fishing break on one of the trout streams on the slopes of Rungwe Mountain in Tukuyu District, I received an urgent message from Tukuyu police station that an African had appeared in the station that morning, and was found clasping the flagpole outside the district commissioner's office from which flew the Union Jack, and stated that he was wanted by the *Serkali* (authority/government) and wished to give himself up. I immediately dispatched my trusted Pathan sub-inspector to the scene and, sure enough, he was our man. He said he was tired of being pursued across Africa and had decided to place himself at the mercy of the Tanganyikan High Court, which had sentenced him to death some two years previously. He was arrested, charged with escape and placed, in leg irons, in the local prison cells. He duly appeared before the court, where it was decided that the death sentence should be carried out and he was hanged.

Justice had been seen to be done but I wondered whether a degree of compassion might not have been exercised in the case. There were times later when I wondered whether it would not have been kinder to have let the case rest in the pile of undetected offences.

'The Passionate Prawn'
She was small, vulgar and South African, married to a miner on

one of the two reef mines in the Lupa Goldfields area in south-
western Tanganyika. They had two small sons who boarded at the
European school in Mbeya, the provincial capital. 'The Lupa' (as
it was known) still had a small population of assorted Europeans,
Asians and Africans, most of whom were engaged in alluvial
mining activities. Of these, some two hundred were Europeans. It
was a rough-and-ready community, living in mini-Klondike conditions. The South African couple were notorious for their family
quarrels, in which bottles used to fly.

'The Passionate Prawn', as she was known locally, used to seek
sanctuary in the Goldfields Hotel in Chunya, the district headquarters, where she could be sure of free drinks. It was rumoured
that these were in fact 'for services rendered' in the back of her
boxbody car, and that at night she used to bed down her two
small boys in the back of her car while she entertained 'customers'
on the front seat. My encounter with the lady was of a rather
more prosaic nature. I was on a police inspection visit to Chunya,
during which I had to deal with a double indecent assault committed by an ex-police superintendent (also employed on one of
the mines) on two middle-aged ladies who respectively managed a
dress shop and a flower shop. These took place mid-morning and
could only have been the result of a mental aberration or excessive
bottled-up virility on the part of the ex-police superintendent.

The 'affairs' were settled amicably when he agreed to apologize
personally to each of the aggrieved ladies and present them with
boxes of chocolates. My wife and I had a luncheon date with the
Resident magistrate, who was a good friend of mine, at the Goldfields Hotel and were much relieved at the break. However, on
arrival at the hotel bar we were confronted by 'The Passionate
Prawn' and her two small boys who were already several days late
for the new term at their boarding school in Mbeya. The mother
was very much the worse for wear after several gins. Ill-advisedly,
I suggested that we might take her two small sons back to school
when I returned to Mbeya that afternoon. She readily agreed,
adding that it would be nice if I were to take her and her dog, a
large, rather dirty Alsatian, as well. To this I demurred, pleading
lack of space in the car. Shortly after lunch with the Resident
magistrate, we collected the two boys, gave them a solid meal

(they looked half-starved and terrified) at our home in Mbeya and delivered them safely to the headmaster at the school.

The sequel to this Good Samaritan act was unexpected. The following morning I received an urgent telephone call from the district commissioner in Chunya, to say that 'The Passionate Prawn' had sent a telegram to the governor of Tanganyika in Dar es Salaam accusing me of kidnapping her two children. The district commissioner required an explanation. However, reinforced by the testimony of my friend and luncheon companion, the Resident magistrate, I was able to refute the allegation and 'The Passionate Prawn' had to admit that her complaint was a fabrication. Had I agreed to take her and her dog as well to Mbeya the previous day, perhaps there would have been no kidnap allegation — but who knows what other charge she might have made?

Caledonian dinner — upcountry style
Scotsmen throughout the world celebrate St Andrew's night in traditional style, and upcountry East Africa was no exception. Wherever two or more Scots could gather together on 30 November, a nucleus existed for a dinner, and Sassenachs and others would enthusiastically rally to the cause. Kilts, where they existed, would be donned, whisky would be stockpiled, and even haggis would be imported at great expense or concocted by loyal Scottish wives for the occasion. The formalities would be observed, a quaich or two would be found for toasts, a chieftain nominated for the occasion and invitations to other 'tribes' would be generously distributed.

One such annual celebration upcounty in Tanganyika in 1946 followed an unusual and, at times, dramatic course. It was a provincial occasion and the organizers had arranged for it to take place in the one hotel in Mbeya. It was a 'black tie' function, with kilts *de rigueur* for the true Scots. Some sixty participants, including a number from the Lupa Goldfields, which were about 50 miles away over a tortuous mountain road, gathered at the appointed time for the usual pre-dinner round(s) of drinks.

The 'chieftain' happened that year to be an old-time 'digger' from the Lupa, who arrived, under friendly escort, the worse for wear from drink. However, all went well until we were summoned to the dinner table and the 'chieftain' was called upon to say grace. He stood up (just), pronounced grace — and then passed out cold on the dinner table. After the body had been removed to one of the hotel bedrooms, the celebrations continued successfully and noisily until the 'wee small hours'. As provincial superintendent of police, I discreetly withdrew from the proceedings shortly after midnight and walked home.

I was woken with some difficulty in the early hours, suffering from a monumental hangover, by a call from the police station to the effect that a police patrol had found the body of a large European in a ditch and would I come to the scene post-haste. I hurried out in some disarray to find the provincial veterinary officer unconscious in the ditch. Again it was necessary to remove the body — this time to his home and an anxious wife. In addition to the after-effects of excessive alcohol, he was suffering from a black eye and a very bruised jaw.

When he was able to talk, it transpired that at the end of the celebrations, on his way home, he had been involved in a heated argument with a junior member of the administration and they had slugged it out, black ties and all, until he was felled and then dumped by his opponent in the ditch. Apart from a friendly admonition on the inconvenience he had caused by failing to get home intact, he was left to sleep off the effects of his encounter. His adversary retreated to his district headquarters in Chunya, on the Lupa, the same morning, ashamed and chastened after a torrid session with the provincial commissioner. In both cases, their careers in the colonial service came to a premature end a few years later.

Handing and taking over (Iringa)
Like any public service, the colonial police had its share of mavericks. In Tanganyika, at the end of the Second World War, there were some police officers who were more distinguished for their eccentricities than their professionalism.

After a war spent largely in the intelligence services, I welcomed the opportunity to assume charge of my first independent district police command. This was in an upcountry station, covering a

141

district the size of Scotland with a population of some 350,000. It was an unusual district in that, in addition to the largely rural African population, there were some 200 European farmers (tea, tobacco and mixed farms) and traders, plus a sizeable Italian mission presence of the *consolata* order.

To police this area and population, I was assisted by a Sikh inspector (whom I subsequently prosecuted for corruption), an African sub-inspector (who was eventually discharged for persistent drunkenness), an African sergeant-major and 50 other ranks. The district headquarters was housed in an old nineteenth-century German fort and there were five substations scattered over the district. On arrival, filled with enthusiasm for the task, I enquired from the officer whom I was relieving, who was known locally as 'Louis the Rocket', when it would be convenient to complete the formalities on handing and taking over the district command. He brushed this aside as being unnecessary and said that he was personally concerned at leaving the district as soon as convenient. I reminded him that, although I could not force him to observe and conform with the regulations, if there were any deficiencies or shortcomings, I would not be responsible and that he would have to answer for them. He accepted this, packed his bags and left the district. I proceeded with the inspection of the facilities and resources available to me in my new task.

On the first day, when checking the armoury and stores, I was confronted with a bolted and padlocked door, which led to a dungeon-like room in the basement of the fort. None of the officers or NCOs were prepared to unlock the door. They told me it was known as the *chumba cha maiti* (room of the corpses). Since no Christian or Muslim officer was prepared to unlock the padlock, I suggested it had best be done by either a pagan or myself. A pagan constable volunteered to carry out the task and I entered a damp, mouldy cell-like room which appeared to be empty. However, in a corner on a plinth lay a sack. I instructed the constable to collect it and reveal the contents. To my surprise, it contained the remains of two humans, with skulls, teeth and bones in remarkably good condition.

It was then divulged that, some months earlier, two Masai had been killed in an interclan fight and the dead bodies were brought in to the district police headquarters. There was some difficulty in establishing the identity of those responsible for their deaths and witnesses were not readily forthcoming, so my predecessor ordered the remains of the two dead men to be stored away in a sack and forgotten.

Subsequently, it was discovered that a number of unnatural deaths had not been reported to the coroner and that, in at least two cases, bodies had been disinterred and disposed of without exhumation orders. It was little wonder that 'Louis the Rocket' showed marked reluctance to complete the handing and taking over formalities. True to my word, I had no alternative but to report these omissions; 'Louis the Rocket' received his 'rocket' — though remained for some more years in the service without promotion — and the skulls and bones of the forgotten Masai were dispatched to the medical school in Dar es Salaam, it is hoped for instructional use.

The 'thunderbox'

In the absence of waterborne sanitation in many upcountry or 'bush' stations in Africa after the last war, we were all dependent on the pit latrine or the 'thunderbox' (commode) for necessary daily relief. All those who served in these stations will be familiar with the inevitable hazards in the use of the 'thunderbox', snakes in the thatched roof, scorpions and hornets in the walls and the occasional unwelcome 'intruder' under the seat. Three notable incidents exemplifying these hazards come to mind.

At the beginning of the war, at the police training depot in Dar es Salaam, there was one of these 'conveniences' sited by the parade ground for the use of inspecting officers and drill and weapon training instructors. An archetypal ex-Guards sergeant-major filled the role of drill and weapon training instructor, and ritually retired to the 'thunderbox' at the end of the morning parade. He was all of 18 stone in weight, had a traditional waxed moustache and a very foul mouth. He was known by his initials, 'WWW'.

One morning after parade, I was roused from my office by yells and unrepeatable expletives to find WWW beating a hasty and undignified retreat from his perch with his ample shorts around his ankles. He was in a state of high agitation, and claimed that he had been bitten by a snake while on the 'throne'. We hurried to the scene while a search was made for snakebite serum. When we arrived at the 'thunderbox' it was only to find that a hen had established herself in the nest in the pan and was in the process of laying an egg when confronted with WWW's massive haunches — so she pecked him sharply. WWW was spared a second injection.

A similar situation arose during the war in an upcountry hotel in Uganda, where guests were obliged to queue after breakfast until a hen had been removed from the comfort of what she understandably believed to be her nesting box.

The most embarrassing incident happened to me personally in Iringa, in Tanganyika, after the war, when I paid an early morning call to our 'thunderbox', which was sited in the garden about 50 yards from the house. I had just settled down when I heard a sinister rustling in the pan. I jumped up to investigate, thinking it might be a snake, only to be confronted with the cheerful face of the African nightsoil collector who had arrived early on his clearance round. He greeted me, apologized profusely, withdrew his head and left me to complete my interrupted 'devotions'.

Pecking order

A curious facet of life in the colonial service in the immediate postwar years was the survival of the feudal pattern of government service. This was reflected in the status of the provincial administration, rather unaffectionately known as 'the heaven-born', and the professional and social grading of other departmental officers. Most, though not all, officers of the provincial administration were university graduates, usually with a public school background, and professional officers such as those in the agricultural, medical, veterinary and legal departments were conceded the right to consider themselves second only to the administration.

For some inexplicable reason, police officers were not accorded professional status, despite training and experience and, in a few instances, a university background. Public works and technical officers were treated as if they were at the bottom of the pile. I suspect that these anomalies derived from social snobbery rather than lack of appreciation of the need and undoubted value of departmental services.

This was best exemplified in a strange manner. African women prisoners, usually serving short custodial sentences for illicit brewing and assaults, were employed in extramural labour such as cutting firewood. Every week a prison warder would arrive in the morning at one's house accompanied by a small group of women prisoners bearing loads of firewood, which was delivered free to government officials. The district commissioner would receive six loads, the district officer four and department officers three each. As far as I was aware, officers in the public works department and others in the bottom grade received nothing. This was an example of petty and unnecessary discrimination, which clearly did little to stimulate *esprit de corps* but was typical of an era that bore little resemblance to reality in an already changing world.

The ninth green (Iringa)

Expatriates in small upcountry communities in post-Second World War Tanganyika were few in number and, inevitably, were largely interdependent socially. Life was full and everyone was busy during working hours. Social amenities were limited, though in some stations much was done to make leisure hours tolerable. We were fortunate in living in a district centre where there were two hotels (one owned by the railways, the other by a Greek) and a club. The Greek-owned hotel bore the improbable name of The White Horse Inn.

Apart from the official community of administrators, medical, agricultural, public works and police staff, there were a number of expatriate tobacco, maize and tea farmers, a bank manager, railways and road service engineers, and even an elderly German barber. The club boasted a tennis court and a nine-hole golf course. Social life revolved around the two hotels and the clubhouse, and there seemed to be an unwritten rule that one of them should be the venue for a party almost every evening in the week. Shortly after our arrival, we were uprooted from our beds one night and bidden to join a party at the Greek hotel. When I protested to the district commissioner the next morning I was told that to refuse would be considered snobbish.

145

Appendix D

'Shipboard' affairs are inevitable in an isolated European community and, during our stay in the district, there were no less than five illegitimate European births. Two dramatic sequels to these affairs come to mind. A very prominent ex-army brigadier who farmed in the district had 'acquired' an attractive English-born wife of an Italian doctor during his service in Somalia during the war. She was at least twenty years his junior and much in demand socially. She was a fair tennis player and used to participate in clubhouse mixed doubles once a week. We all wondered when she would succumb to the attentions of one of several much younger bachelors in the district. Sure enough, during a weekly tennis session, she informed me that she was eloping that evening with a very likeable, virile young Syrian farmer and that her suitcase was packed and in the clubhouse. He duly appeared, we had two or three 'celebratory' drinks in the bar and she left for his farm.

The sequel was most embarrassing. As the only European police officer in the district, I was expected, *inter alia*, to act as a social and domestic counsellor, and was summoned by the cuckolded brigadier to his office the next morning, asked if I knew what had happened and what I could do to persuade his inamorata to return. Apart from making sympathetic noises, I made it clear that this was outside my police duties, whereupon the brigadier dissolved into tears. Happily, some months afterwards, his estranged wife rejoined him and they lived contentedly until his death a few years later.

The climax to the other incident took place on the ninth green at midnight at the district club. Here the scenario was reversed. The German wife of a local British farmer deserted him and moved in to live with a retired major, who had been gaoled and then cashiered from the forces for 'winning' a theodolite from army stores. The major, who was very popular, personable and a regular *habitué* of the club, took it all in his stride and provided a home for his woman and her small boy. All went well for some months, but on one Saturday evening the ex-husband and lover met in the bar of the club. We did our best to keep them apart, but just before the bar closed there was a confrontation. It was decided that, rather than have a punch-up in the bar in front of all the other club members and their wives, they should be shepherded outside. The climax on this occasion was a slugging match on the ninth green by moonlight, with the club members watching the conflict and urging on the contestants. When bloodshed, if not worse, appeared inevitable, I intervened, persuaded them both that honour had been satisfied and packed them off to their respective homes.

Though these incidents were relatively rare, it might be said that they were symptomatic of an isolated social life and of the apparent insensitivity of the Europeans to the impact they might have on the Africans we administered, who were all too aware of the curious conduct of their 'masters'.

The Christmas box and other goodwill gifts

Generally speaking, East Africa in the colonial era was remarkably free of corruption. The popular explanation was that affluence, *per se*, was limited both in the numbers of the rich and the scale of wealth. I like to think that it was mainly due to the high standard of integrity of expatriate public servants and, as a result, to their realization that little or nothing was to be gained by bribery. There were exceptions, as always, and much depended on the philosophy of those who, because of the nature of their professions, were exposed to possible corruption.

A traditional and time-honoured practice was the Asian traders' 'Christmas box'. Almost all wholesale and retail trade, particularly in upcountry stations, was in the hands of Asians (Hindus, Ismaili Muslims and Punjabis) or Arabs. It was acceptable to exact discount from one's grocer, with whom one had been dealing throughout the year, with a bottle of spirits or sherry — depending on the scale of the account — at Christmas. However, this lent itself to abuse, as I was to learn at my first upcountry district command, when a prominent retailer appeared at my house with a box of gifts — whisky, wine, chocolates and cakes — just before Christmas. I had only just arrived at the station and had not yet opened an account with him. I refused point blank to accept the gift, whereupon he produced a book with the names of all the officials and other prominent expatriates in the district, itemizing their gifts and bearing their signatures of receipt. I reminded him that I was not interested in those who had benefited from his largesse, and sent him packing. The following Christmas, after a year's expenditure at his shop, I accepted a bottle of whisky as discount on what he had overcharged me over the previous 12 months.

On another occasion, a well-known Arab fruit and vegetable farmer, who was under investigation for fraud, sent a truck-load of fruit and vegetables to the district police headquarters as a 'goodwill' gesture. I summoned the station staff, mustered all the witnesses and complainants in the vicinity of the station, and announced that the Arab farmer must be a man of wealth as he had sent a truck-load of produce to be distributed to the poor. To their surprise, all those present received free fruit and vegetables on that day. I was never bothered with attempted bribery after that date.

Appendix E

The Sanya Corridor Incident: A Shameful Chapter in the History of Tanganyika

In 1952, the government of Tanganyika appointed a committee of three, comprising the member for lands and mines, the Northern Province veterinary officer and a well-known local Afrikaner farmer to advise on what proved to be a controversial and potentially disastrous project.

The so-called Sanya corridor was a belt of Meru tribal land between stock farms occupied by European settlers. Local pressure was exerted to create a buffer zone in the area between Mt Kilimanjaro and Mt Meru, free of cattle disease which was prevalent among the tribal herds. This would involve the total eviction of 2000 Meru men, women and children and the subsequent lease of the land to expatriate farmers. The government believed that, with compensation and resettlement of the Meru, this could be achieved amicably. It was to be sorely disillusioned. The project received approval from Dar es Salaam and the Northern provincial authorities were authorized to proceed with its implementation. As the Northern region's assistant commissioner of police, I had overall responsibility to ensure that the eviction was carried out peacefully, with care, patience and compassion.

As a prelude to action, the provincial commissioner decided to hold a *baraza* (open meeting) with the elders and tribesmen in the disputed area. Police intelligence indicated that feelings were running high among the Meru and I insisted that the PC and his party should be discreetly covered by two sections of police in Land-Rovers. I decided to accompany the party.

On our arrival at the rendezvous in the Sanya corridor, we were faced with a sullen crowd of tribesmen, fronted by their elders. The PC then made a prepared speech, outlining the background and reasons for the eviction, concluding with a deadline for the move when government officers and transport would be available to assist in the resettlement. Nothing was said until the senior elder stood up. He then bent down to pick up a handful of soil, saying, 'This is our mother and father and you are depriving us of our heritage,' whereupon the crowd started to shout abuse and jostle each other to come closer to the official party. Reluctantly, the PC accepted my advice to withdraw and return to Arusha, rather than face an increasingly hostile mob.

Plans were then made to move government officers (administrative, agricultural and veterinary) into the area, with a sizeable police contingent to protect and enforce the eviction. A camp was established and transport and labour drafted in for the physical move of the tribesmen and their chattels. Since the numbers of Meru were considerable and scattered over a large area, the eviction had to be carried out gradually with the minimum of force.

As the authorities moved in, it was realized that we were dealing with a hostile and uncooperative group of tribesmen and the process was slow and difficult. It was obvious from the outset that everyone involved in carrying out the eviction found it distasteful and unpleasant. The whole operation took several weeks and by the time it was completed there was no sign of human occupation in the Sanya corridor.

Apart from the physical removal of the Meru, their families, stock and personal belongings, all huts and *manyattas* were destroyed by burning, rendering the area an unoccupied wasteland. To the credit of all involved in this very unpleasant project, there were no casualties or injuries, though one Meru woman suffered a miscarriage in the exodus.

The legacy of this arbitrary and apparently unnecessary operation was the creation a sense of injustice among the Meru tribe as a whole, a political protest to the United Nations led by Kirilo

Japhet, a local Meru politician, a worsening of relations between the Meru and the provincial administration and, some years later, a public admission by the then governor, Sir Edward Twining, prior to his retirement, that a major mistake during his tenure of office in Tanganyika had been to sanction the eviction of the Meru from the Sanya corridor.

For a few years, a handful of British and Greek farmers leased and farmed the land in the corridor and, happily, by independence in 1961, the land was restored to the Meru.

Appendix F
Anguilla: A Decolonization Fiasco

Anguilla is an island of 35 square miles, situated 69 miles northwest of St Kitts in the eastern Caribbean. The majority of its population, some 6000, consists of peasant farmers and fishermen and their families. At the beginning of the nineteenth century, together with St Kitts and Nevis, it was part of the British Leeward Islands Federation; again from 1958 to 1962, these three islands constituted part of the abortive West Indies Federation.

Anguilla continued to be administered by St Kitts but was palpably neglected. Apart from a 'warden', appointed by the St Kitts government, and a small police detachment, few or no resources, economic or otherwise, were available to this small geographically detached island. In February 1967, after five years of undefined and generally neglected status, under the West Indies Act, passed by the British Parliament, St Kitts–Nevis–Anguilla became a state in 'voluntary association' with Great Britain. Anguilla continued to exist as an out-island component, without a town, village or organized centre for the population, with no electricity, gas, telephones or adequate water supply and with roads no better than dirt tracks. Most able-bodied young Anguillans had long left the island to seek employment in the US Virgin Islands (St Thomas, St Croix), Dutch or French St Martin (the island's closest neighbour), Puerto Rico, or even further afield in the USA or

Britain. (There is a sizeable Anguillan community in Slough, west of London.)

Resentment against the perpetuation of the link with St Kitts under the West Indies Act was general on the island and, in June 1967, it came to a head when 250 islanders (some of whom were armed) rebelled, burnt down the warden's house and forced the dozen police on the island to flee to St Kitts. Telecommunications between Anguilla and St Kitts were cut.

Premier Robert Bradshaw of the 'Associated State' of St Kitts, Nevis and Anguilla declared the revolt illegal (which, of course, in legalistic terms, it was) and asked Britain to send troops to quell it. On 11 July 1967, Anguilla held a referendum on its continued association with St Kitts–Nevis. By 1813 votes to 5, it chose independence, thus refuting the St Kitts contention that the rebellion was the work of a small minority. In the same month, representatives of Great Britain, Barbados, Trinidad and Guyana met in Barbados in an attempt to end Anguilla's secession. Bradshaw signed an agreement which, although it stipulated the return of Anguilla to constitutional relations with St Kitts–Nevis, provided for a local council. The arrangement, which was an unrealistic compromise, was short-lived.

Peter Adams, the only Anguillan MP in the three-island legislature, was replaced by a well-known local personality, Ronald Webster, a Seventh-Day Adventist pastor and businessman. Under his leadership, Anguilla reaffirmed its desire for independence. Great Britain, with no resident diplomatic representation in St Kitts, was poorly informed of developments.

In December 1967, Anthony Lee, a former colonial official in Africa, was appointed for 12 months as administrator 'to act in a liaison capacity between Anguilla and St Kitts'. Apart from his dubious constitutional status in a quasi-independent associated state, his role could, at best, be described as that of an adviser. In the interim, visits were paid to the island by two British MPs and letters were exchanged between Lord Shepherd, the Minister of State at the Foreign and Commonwealth Office, and Bradshaw and Webster respectively.

With no sign of an easing of the tension in sight, Bradshaw and Webster attended talks in London in October 1968 when a permanent solution and an extension of the interim settlement were discussed. No agreement was reached on the former and, after further correspondence following the talks, Webster claimed that, with the expiry of the interim settlement on 31 December 1968, Anguilla would revert to 'full independence and freedom of action'. As Anguilla's status was governed by the West Indies Act of 1967, HMG considered Webster's declaration of no effect. Meanwhile, in January 1969, Anthony Lee left Anguilla and development aid, administered through him, ceased. Based on Antigua, he continued to pay periodic visits to the island — 'to enable HM Government to discharge the responsibilities of external affairs and defence' (residual powers entrusted to Britain in an associated state). In reality the impasse was complete. During these visits, Lee became aware of the increasing influence on Webster of several US citizens, led by Jack Holcomb, who had managed a private detective agency in the USA. Another American, Goudge, a Baptist minister who had lived in Anguilla for four years, was alleged to have been involved to a lesser degree. There were also unsubstantiated reports of arms smuggling and Mafia interest in the island as a potential gambling centre.

In effect, with little firm intelligence and the isolation resulting from the 'secession', rumours of hostile or undesirable influences were rife. Such was the position prior to the visit of Mr William Whitlock MP, the parliamentary under-secretary for Foreign and Commonwealth Affairs, in March 1969. He bore with him a message from the British prime minister, Harold Wilson, explaining what action would be taken 'in the interests of the people of Anguilla'. This included, *inter alia*:

- the appointment of a civil commissioner by HM the Queen. Tony Lee was specifically designated for the task — 'as you already know him well and he understands your problems and aspirations' (*sic*);
- the appointment of an advisory committee to assist HM commissioner;
- the appointment of a magistrate for Anguilla;
- the establishment of a grant-in-aid by HMG to bridge the gap between taxation and expenditure;

- the establishment of a land registry; and
- no prosecutions for political activities during the previous 21 months.

From the foregoing, it will be noted that there was no mention of the main bone of contention, namely the link in statehood with St Kitts–Nevis. The last of the above proposals was interpreted by Anguillans as a meaningless 'amnesty'.[1]

The events of Tuesday 11 March 1969

During the first week of March 1969, Mr Whitlock and his advisers had been visiting other Caribbean leaders prior to his mission to Anguilla. In my capacity as overseas police adviser to the Secretary of State for Foreign and Commonwealth Affairs, I was on a routine visit to the police forces of the eastern Caribbean to advise on reorganization, development and training programmes. I met the minister and his staff fortuitously in Antigua and was asked if I would accompany the party to Anguilla. I suggested that because there was no recognized police force on the island, there would be little point in doing so, but added that if the minister thought I could be of assistance, I would gladly accompany the party. I then put the matter out of my mind and continued with the tour of forces in the Windward Islands.

Five days later I was informed, when in St Vincent, that I should proceed forthwith to join the minister's party in Antigua. On arrival in Antigua, on 10 March, I joined a full meeting of the minister and his advisers at the Barrymore Hotel in St John's, Antigua. The party consisted of Mr Whitlock, Roland Hunt, the assistant under-secretary at the FCO responsible for Caribbean affairs, Tony Rushford, an FCO legal counsellor, Stuart Roberts, the British government representative to the associated states, Tony Williams, a British embassy counsellor in Washington,

---

1. Lee, who knew the island intimately, advised the FCO against the visit but was overruled. Before the ministerial visit was finalized, he was contacted on the telephone by the deputy under-secretary of state in the Foreign Office and was asked bluntly (and naïvely), 'Old boy, are you for or against us?' Such was the lack of confidence in the man on the spot.

Desmond Kerr, assistant BGR to the associated states, Robin Gorham, PS to the minister, Major Peter Ferguson, Royal Marines, and an inspector (Smith) and sergeant (Waller) from Scotland Yard, who were to provide close escort protection for the minister. Tony Lee had travelled to Anguilla the previous day and sent an encouraging message by radio on the mood of the islanders and the reception the minister would be likely to receive.

In the meantime, in preparation for the minister's visit, contingency plans included the transfer of the diplomatic wireless service unit from the Barrymore Hotel to Anguilla and the stationing, 'hull-down over the horizon', of the Royal Navy frigate HMS *Minerva*, with 14 Royal Marines on board, out of sight but with radio communication to the DWS unit, and a helicopter available, in case the minister's party required immediate assistance or rescue. Thus, the ground had been prepared for the worst. As will be seen later in the narrative, these well-laid plans, in the event, proved disastrously ineffective.

At 12.15 p.m. on Tuesday 11 March 1969, the minister and his party (less Anthony Williams and Desmond Kerr) left Antigua airport in a chartered aircraft, scheduled to arrive in Anguilla at 12.50 p.m. Despite Tony Lee's reassuring message of the previous day, it was thought possible that extremists on the island might endeavour to block the airstrip, so, before landing, a visual check through binoculars was made to ensure that it was clear. There were no obstructions and we duly landed smoothly and safely.

The scene that greeted us was remarkable — a crowd of some 500 Anguillans, men, women and children, had assembled at the airstrip, waving pro-British banners and Union Jacks. Our arrival was cheered and the national anthem was sung several times. Upon disembarkation from the aircraft, the minister was received by Tony Lee and Ronald Webster with whom we shook hands in an aura of cordiality. Webster, who was accompanied by a group of close supporters, was formally dressed in a black suit, frilly-fronted shirt and white gloves. This too was the 'funeral parlour garb' of his close associates. The ministerial party, escorted by Webster and his colleagues, then pushed their way through the apparently happy crowd to the veranda of the airport building where Webster delivered a mild speech of welcome, calling on the islanders to make the minister's stay as enjoyable and safe as possible.

Whitlock then delivered his prepared speech, which was received enthusiastically by the crowd. He then announced that he would be touring the island that afternoon and on succeeding days to explain to the islanders precisely what the British government had in mind for Anguilla. Large numbers of a leaflet containing the contents of the British government's offer were distributed and thrown like chicken feed to the crowd.

The first hitch then occurred. Lee had arranged for the minister to stay during the visit at the house of Mr Henry Howard, a former British colonial administrator (of St Kitts) who had retired to Anguilla but who, at the time, was absent in Puerto Rico. Lee had arranged transport to take us directly from the airport to Sandy Hill Bay, which was about three and a half miles to the east of the airstrip. The house had been leased to Gerald Siefert, a young Canadian, who was the local bank manager. He was a bachelor and was to be the minister's host during the stay in Anguilla. The rest of us would be billeted at various houses on the island. The diplomatic wireless service team were to be based some seven miles from the minister's headquarters at Sandy Hill Bay. As there were no telephones on the island, the only means of direct communication between the minister and his party and the outside world (including HMS *Minerva*, the Royal Navy frigate) through the DWS radio link, would be by car over an unmade dirt track, by cycle or on foot (shades of the 'cleft stick').

Second, it was evident on our departure from the airstrip that Webster and, in particular Jeremiah Gumbs, his most militant supporter and the owner of the Rendezvous Hotel, had expected us to proceed first to the hotel and lunch before touring the island. A convoy of cars had been laid on and, on departure for Howard's house, we literally left Webster and company standing. Resentment was obvious but, inexplicably, ignored. In the meantime, we all settled in at Sandy Hill Bay, enjoyed an excellent lunch provided by Mrs Emile Gumbs, the Canadian wife of a local moderate and friend of Mr Siefert.

At 2.40 p.m. I accompanied Messrs Lee, Hunt and Roberts to contact Atlin Harrison, another prominent moderate and editor of the local broadsheet. On arrival, he immediately expressed alarm at Webster's reaction to the minister's visit and warned us to expect trouble. We hastened back to Sandy Hill Bay and the minister to alert him. In our absence, ironically, Siefert had left with a signal from the minister for transmission by the DWS team to HMS *Minerva* to the effect that he had arrived safely on the island. The tour of the island by the ministerial party was due to start at 3.15 p.m. and was to end at 4.00 p.m. at the community centre where he would address the islanders.

On our return from visiting Atlin Harrison, we found a chain had been stretched across the entrance drive to the Sandy Hill Bay house and large boulders placed across the track so that no vehicles could leave. The roadblock was manned by four islanders on cycles, wearing mining helmets, and one had an M1 carbine slung over his shoulder. We were told in no uncertain (racially abusive) terms that no one could leave until 'de President' (Webster) had first spoken to Mr Whitlock. We duly proceeded on foot and briefed the minister on what appeared to be an alarmingly dangerous situation.

At 3.40 p.m. Lee, Inspector Smith and I visited the barrier and demanded that it be removed. There were now 12 men at the roadblock and one was armed with an automatic pistol, strapped to his thigh. While we were arguing, Webster arrived, still dressed in his funeral parlour garb and carrying a briefcase. We escorted him down the drive and Lee only broke the silence to comment on the fine weather, to which there was no response from Webster. On arrival at the house, the minister reminded Webster of the dangerous situation he was creating by using force against an HMG minister and demanded the removal of the barrier and his armed men so that he could proceed with his programme.

Webster's reaction was to present the minister with a printed ultimatum of his demands, obviously prepared well in advance of the visit, which amounted to the complete independence of Anguilla. He also demanded that the minister and his party should leave within half an hour, as he could not guarantee their safety. He then left, escorted by Lee and the inspector of police, to join his supporters at the roadblock. It was now obvious that we had fallen into a trap. Tension began to build up and it was noticed that a crowd was gathering in force on a ridge about 300 yards from our base. Careful observation was kept on the approach road and on the ridge and, by 4.30 p.m., at least four rifle-armed men were identified in the crowd.

At 5.00 p.m. the two taxi drivers, who had been employed to transport us to Sandy Hill Bay, had walked up the drive and had been told to inform Mr Whitlock that we must leave the house within ten minutes. The taxi drivers indicated that they too were reluctant to remain. Ten minutes later, Police Sergeant Ryan, who 'commanded' Webster's small unofficial force of 'Keystone Cops', accompanied by a local constable, came down the drive and stated that he wished to speak to Mr Whitlock. Inspector Smith firmly told him that this would not be permitted and that any message he had would be relayed to Whitlock by the inspector. Sergeant Ryan said that the DWS radio operators and their equipment were at the airfield, that the minister's safety could no longer be guaranteed and that everyone should leave at once.

When informed, Whitlock came out of the house and joined us. Smith passed on the message to Whitlock who asked the sergeant if he could speak again with Webster. He was told he could walk up the drive and speak to 'de President' at the roadblock. Ryan was informed by Inspector Smith that, as the minister's safety could no longer be guaranteed, this was out of the question and that Webster should be brought down to the house. At this point, eight men, some carrying small arms, came down the drive and joined us. Ryan then shouted across to the ridge for Webster and blew his whistle to attract attention. The reply was several shots, obviously not from the same weapon, fired in our direction. Two shots were fired from close range from the undergrowth around the house. They appeared to be from an automatic weapon.

No sound of passing bullets was heard and it was impossible to say whether the shots had been fired at us directly or over our heads. We then withdrew, without undignified haste, into the house. Clearly, a crisis point had been reached and Lee advised the minister that, if it were decided to remain, the least that could happen would be an attempt to burn down the house after nightfall, risking the lives of our host, the Gumbs and the domestic staff. Mr Whitlock gave the order for us to depart. The two taxi drivers were anxiously awaiting withdrawal, so we made our fare-wells and left in convoy for the airfield. On departure, it was evident that we should have run the gauntlet as we passed Webster's base on the ridge, so Inspector Smith and I flanked Mr Whitlock in the back of our taxi to provide some physical protection against possible missiles and abuse. We kept the windows open for fear of flying glass and relied on our, as yet untested, skills as 'fielders' of stones.'

The convoy was stopped on the track at the landward end of 'Webster's Ridge' where 'de President' could be seen directing operations. He had ordered our cars to be stopped so that we could be provided with an 'escort' of cars and lorries containing his jeering supporters. No firearms of any kind were visible. At the airstrip, a crowd of about 150 had assembled — in a very different mood from the one that had welcomed us earlier in the day. There were very few women and it was obvious that Webster had brought every follower he could to the airstrip.

Two Cessna six-seater Apache aircraft belonging to the firm of Valley Air Services, which normally ran the shuttle service between Dutch St Maarten and Anguilla, had been held at the airstrip to provide onward transport. The DWS radio operators with their equipment were already at the airstrip when we arrived. They recounted that at about 3.00 p.m. they had been visited by Sergeant Ryan and a constable who had informed them that Webster had said that their safety could not be guaranteed and that they should pack up and leave. They ignored the warning but at 4.00 p.m. the sergeant, constable and about twenty supporters, some carrying arms, returned to enforce the ultimatum.

The DWS operators packed up their equipment, but not before managing to send a radio message to HMS *Minerva* that they were being force to close down by an armed gang. Apparently, the three operators were treated in a friendly manner by those at the airstrip until Webster and his followers arrived about 30 minutes later, when a moderate in the crowd was savagely beaten and kicked. The ministerial party arrived at 5.40 p.m. and our baggage was quickly loaded onto the aircraft to the accompaniment of jeers, insults and obscenities, and with the exception of Lee and Inspector Smith, we departed for St Maarten, some eight miles away.

Meanwhile, on Anguilla, Gerald Siefert, our host, who had accompanied us to the airfield, had been threatened by Webster's men; he decided to leave with the 'rearguard' of Lee and Smith and to close down the bank. After the departure of the main party, the crowd at the airfield became increasingly restless and insults and obscenities continued. At one stage, Inspector Smith was surrounded by a group and identified to the others as the 'gunslinger'. Fortunately, he had handed his gun to me when I boarded the second aircraft for St Maarten. At 6.20 p.m. Lee and Smith boarded an aircraft for St Maarten, but Siefert was told by Webster, who offered hotel accommodation and a guard, that he would have to remain on the island. Siefert did not demur and agreed to this arrangement.

Meanwhile, the arrival of the main party at St Maarten airport aroused considerable local and press interest. The siege of Sandy Hill Bay had already been broadcast to the world and at least two 'stringers' from American news agencies were awaiting us, anxious for details of events on the island. Unfortunately, no one had prepared an agreed statement on events and the minister and other members of the party had to fend off questions with *ad hoc* answers. This, to my mind, was a major communications error, which led to garbled and entirely inaccurate versions of what had really happened.

What had been the makings of a dangerous crisis was portrayed by the press as a farce compounded by mismanagement. The depth of antagonism in Anguilla to the artificial hotchpotch 'Associated State' of St Kitts–Nevis–Anguilla and, in particular, to the premier, Robert Bradshaw, had been underestimated, as had been the militancy of Ronald Webster and his Anguillan supporters. Old-fashioned paternalism no longer cut any ice. We were all safely back in Antigua that night to lick our injured pride if not our wounds. A full 'wash-up' meeting, presided over by Whitlock, was held the next morning in Antigua and, apart from Tony Lee, Tony Rushford, the FCO legal adviser, Inspector Smith, Sergeant Waller and myself, the minister's party left that afternoon for London, leaving the five of us to conduct a detailed inquest into the events of 11 March and to endeavour to identify the leaders of the 'rebellion'. On 13 March we returned to London, arriving in the early hours of 14 March, leaving Tony Lee in Antigua as a rear link. By midday I had been summoned to the Cabinet Office to find HMG in the throes of mounting a major military operation against Webster's rebellion. Though subsequent actions received disproportionate world publicity and are well known, a short chronicle of events in the next two years is worth recording.

On 19 March 1969, after a formal request from the premier of St Kitts–Nevis–Anguilla, Britain gave the order for troops to move to Anguilla. The use of the Parachute Regiment, though wholly effective and meeting no resistance from the Anguillans, appeared to be using a sledgehammer to crack a nut. The operation would have been equally effective with a small group of Royal Marines or SAS. A storm of criticism followed and, in retrospect, it may be said that the psychological damage to Britain's reputation far exceeded any success in Anguilla.

Ronald Webster immediately demanded Tony Lee's withdrawal (Lee had been reinstated as administrator) and Lord Caradon, Britain's representative at the United Nations, was called in to negotiate. Shortly afterwards, John Cumber, the former administrator of the Cayman Islands, replaced Lee. A commission of inquiry, presided over by Sir Hugh Wooding, a distinguished West Indies judge, was established to examine the causes and complaints of the Anguillans which had led to the rebellion.

Relative calm was restored and by August 1969 almost all British combat troops had been withdrawn and replaced by 84 Metropolitan Police and a 'heart and minds' contingent of 140 Royal Engineers, the latter deployed on public works projects such as road building and the reconstruction of wharves. The 'occupation forces' were costing the British taxpayer £1 million a year. Eighteen months later (March 1971) only 20 Metropolitan Police and 55 Royal Engineers remained.

By now it was clear that every effort should be made for Anguillans to be given the opportunity to participate much more fully in managing their own affairs and, to this end, I was involved in a programme to 'localize' the small police force on the island. In 1972, a British-trained ex-police commissioner of Anguillan origin was placed in charge of the force. Two years later all personnel in his force were Anguillans.

Anguilla: A Decolonization Fiasco

In June 1971, following a visit by the minister of state in the Foreign and Commonwealth Office, Joseph Godber, Britain reluctantly resumed full and open control of Anguilla, including defence of the island. Webster, who was still the most effective local leader, agreed — despite the combined opposition of all the other eastern Caribbean associate states. Today, all those states have attained independent sovereign status — Anguilla remains a British colony.

It would be churlish to state categorically how Britain's Anguillan dilemma could have been resolved at the time in 1967 when, through the West Indies Act, an attempt was made to guide this patchwork of disparate island units in the eastern Caribbean towards independence. But it should be said that, perhaps, more attention should have been given to the strength of local feeling in these small island communities before slotting in the pieces of a rather untidy jigsaw puzzle.

As to the actual risks inherent in the situation on Anguilla on Tuesday 11 March 1969, when I visited the island on an inspection visit exactly 12 months later in March 1970, the administrator gave a luncheon at his residence where I met some of Webster's gun-toting supporters of 1969, now restored to respectability. In a friendly social discussion, I was told by them that at no time had they intended to attack us at Sandy Hill Bay — the shots fired had been directed over our heads, 'just to show we meant business and that you all should leave the islands — which, of course, is what we did.

Appendix G
Responsibilities of Overseas Police Adviser/Inspector-General of Police, Dependent Territories, Foreign and Commonwealth Office

a) To advise and liaise with the geographical and functional departments of the Foreign and Commonwealth Office, and the Ministry of Overseas Development, and to liaise with the Home Office, the Ministry of Defence and other interested government departments and services on matters relating to assistance and advice to independent Commonwealth and foreign police forces in accordance with HMG's overseas policy.

b) To pay regular (biennial) inspection visits to British dependent territories' police forces (of which there were still 17), and to review the internal security capability of these forces.

c) To ensure close consultation with the Home Office, the Ministry of Overseas Development and United Kingdom police forces and advise on requests for training by overseas governments in UK police training establishments, and to assist in making necessary financial arrangements with the government department or service concerned for both regular and specialist training.

d) To maintain records of overseas police organizations.

e) To ensure liaison with other donor countries (USA, Canada, Australia and West Germany) that have overseas police development and training programmes.

f) To recommend priorities and estimate future requirements of countries requiring UK police development and training assistance.

g) To act as referral point in Whitehall for British police advisory and training missions overseas.

h) To act in support of supervisory staff at British police training establishments (National Police College, Bramshill; Metropolitan Police Training School; and West Yorkshire Police Academy) where courses of training were held for overseas officers and to visit all such establishments regularly.

i) To assist in selection of officers for service overseas.

j) To visit independent Commonwealth and foreign countries at their request and advise on police organizational, operational, training and equipment problems.

k) To ensure constant liaison with the Home Office and the UK police service on new techniques in law enforcement.

l) To participate as a member of the UK delegation in Interpol activities.

m) To act as a central point in Whitehall for all enquiries on overseas police matters in which HMG has an interest.

Liaison with government departments and agencies

Superintending under-secretary, FCO	Direct as necessary
Heads of geographical departments, FCO and ODM	Direct on routine basis
Cabinet Office (assessments staff)	Reports on visits and inspections
ODM recruitment executive	Appointments overseas; selection board
M.o.D (DS and Military Assistance Office)	Reports on visits and inspections paramilitary training programmes; loan personnel and police projects overseas
UKLF Wilton	Periodical review of IS in dependent territories; contingency planning

Procurement executive	Re-employment of ex-overseas police officers
British Council	UK police training programmes; selection and placing of candidates from overseas
Home Office	Consultation with police department and office of chief inspector of constabulary on provision of seconded UK police officers overseas; UK training programmes and work study visits by foreign police officers to the UK; liaison on international narcotics control programmes and training and assistance requests
National Police College, Bramshill	Regular visits; advice and assistance to director of overseas studies; interview overseas trainees
Metropolitan Police	Direct contact (through Home Office) on requests for assistance in crime investigation overseas; regular consultation on overseas training courses conducted at Metropolitan Training School, Peel Centre, Hendon; attendance as inspecting officer at end of course parades; advise and assist supervisory staff (overseas courses) at Hendon
Police authorities throughout the UK	Regular contacts on training programmes and requests; *ad hoc* enquiries; interview overseas trainees
Crown Agents	Recruitment of directly employed police officers overseas; attendance on interview boards; close consultation on equipment, transport and warlike stores; orders from overseas
British Airways/British Caledonian Airways	Airport security attachments for overseas police officers
Department of Trade	Liaison on civil aviation security

Overseas liaison

International Criminal Police Organization (Interpol), Paris	Coordination of representation and channels of communication of dependent territories; as a member of UK delegation, attendance at Annual General Assembly

166

Responsibilities of Overseas Police Adviser

USA — FBI, DEA, US customs service	Exchange of information and coordination of training programmes
Foreign, independent Commonwealth and dependent territories police forces	Regular semi-official correspondence, much of it developed on a personal basis over the 12 years
UN Narcotics Division, Geneva	Direct liaison on UN narcotics training programmes, identification of areas of cooperation, particularly in SE Asia
Inspections and visits overseas	See attached schedule

Visits and inspections (1966–78)
Dependent territories' police forces[1] — inspections

	Mediterranean
Gibraltar	August 1966
	June 1967
	July 1969
	April 1973
	July 1976
	January 1979

	West Indies and Atlantic
Anguilla	March 1969
	April 1969
	November 1969
	December 1973
	May 1976
Ascension Island	November 1973
Belize	November 1966
	December 1969
	November 1971
	October 1974
	October 1978
Bermuda	November 1967
	May 1969
	April 1970

---

1. A total of 19,364 police officers (Hong Kong 16,997) are employed in the following dependent territories. In the years 1966–78 a total of 267 consultancy visits and inspections were carried out, embracing 77 countries/territories.

167

	October 1973
	October 1976
	December 1977
Cayman Islands	February 1967
	March 1967
	July 1970
	April 1972
	January 1974
	November 1975
	December 1977
Falkland Islands	November 1973
Monserrat	November 1966
	February 1969
	November 1969
	March 1971
	April 1972
	October 1974
	May 1976
St Helena	April 1971
	May 1975
Tristan da Cunha	November 1973
Turks & Caicos Islands	February 1967
	March 1969
	July 1970
	April 1972
	January 1974
	June 1976

Hong Kong and Pacific

British Solomon Islands	April 1968
	November 1970
	April 1973
	August 1975
	August 1977
	June 1979
Gilbert Islands	May 1968
	November 1970
	April 1973
(incl. Nauru and Ocean Island)	August 1975
	July 1977
Hong Kong	October 1967
	December 1972
	November 1974
	November/December 1976
New Hebrides	April 1968
	November 1970

	April 1973
	August 1975
	August 1977
	May/June 1979
Tuvalu	May 1968
	August 1975

Independent Commonwealth and foreign countries — visits and consultancies

Mediterranean, Middle and Near East

Cyprus	January 1973 (in transit)
Egypt	August 1968
	June 1971
	January 1973
	April 1974
	January 1976
	January 1978
Iran	May 1973 (in transit)
Lebanon	January 1973
Libya	September 1967

East, central and southern Africa (including Indian Ocean)

Botswana	July 1966
	March 1967
	February 1970
	February 1972
	May 1974
	February 1976
	May 1978
Ethiopia	May 1974 (in transit)
Kenya	August 1966
	February 1970
	July 1971
	February 1972
	January 1973 (in transit)
	May 1974
	April 1978
Lesotho	February 1970
	February 1972
	May 1974
	March 1976
	May 1978
Mauritius	July 1966
	October 1968

	December 1972
	July 1979
Seychelles	August 1966
	June 1970
	January 1972
	January 1973
	March 1976
	December 1976
	July 1979
Swaziland	March 1968
	February 1970
	February 1972
	May 1974
	March 1976
	May 1978
Zambia	February 1972
	February 1976
	April 1978

West Africa

Gambia, The	February 1971
	May 1975
	October 1976
	October/November 1977
	February 1979
Ghana	August 1967
	August 1969
	October 1976
	October/November 1977
	February 1979
Mali	January 1971
Nigeria	August 1967
	August 1969
	October 1972
Senegal	February 1971
Sierra Leone	August 1969
	May 1975
	October 1976
	February 1979

Asia

Afghanistan	May 1973
Bangladesh	August 1972
	March 1975
	July 1977
Indonesia	December 1976

	July 1979
Malaysia	October 1971
	December 1972
	December 1973
	December 1974
	December 1976
	July 1979
Pakistan	May 1973
Sri Lanka	April 1971
	May 1973
	December 1974
	December 1976
Thailand	December 1974
	July 1979

Pacific Ocean

Fiji	May 1968
	October 1970
	March 1973
	July 1975
	July/August 1977
	May/June 1979
Nauru	August 1975
	August 1977
	May 1979
Papua/New Guinea	July 1975
	March 1968
Tonga	June 1968
	October 1970

Arabia

Abu Dhabi	February 1968
	February 1970
Bahrain	February 1968
	February 1970
Dubai	February 1968
	February 1970
	March 1977
Oman	February 1970
	June 1976
	March 1977
PDR of the Yemen (Aden)	March 1972 (in transit)
Qatar	February 1968
	February 1970
Ras el Khaimah	February 1970
Saudi Arabia	February 1970

171

	March 1972
	January 1976
	June 1976
	March 1977
	January 1978
	January 1979
Sharjah	February 1968
	February 1970
Yemen Arab Republic	March 1972
	May 1979

Caribbean

Antigua	November 1966
	February 1969
	November 1969
	March 1971
	May 1973
	December 1973
	May 1976
Bahamas	August 1968
	March 1969
	November 1970
	December 1973
	November 1975 (in transit)
	December 1977
Barbados	November 1966
	November 1969
	March 1971
	December 1973
	May 1976
	February 1977
	November 1978
	April 1979
Dominica	November 1966
	March 1969
	November 1969
	March 1971
Grenada	November 1966
	November 1969
	March 1971
	April 1979
Guyana	November 1966
	November 1978
Jamaica	December 1966
	November 1968
	October 1969

	July 1970
	November 1973
	January 1975
	November 1975
	December 1977
	June and November 1978
St Kitts–Nevis	November 1966
	March 1969
	November 1969
	March 1971
St Lucia	November 1966
	November 1969
	March 1971
	December 1973
	May 1976
	March 1977
St Vincent	November 1966
	March 1969
	October 1969
	March 1971

Interpol conferences

Austria	1973
Belgium	1970
Canada	1971
France	1974
Ghana	1976
Iran	1968
Japan	1967
Mexico	1969
Panama City	1978
Sweden	1977
West Germany	1972

Other conferences and liaison meetings

| USA | Each year from 1966–77 |
| Canada | 1966, 1967, 1970, and each year from 1974–7 |

Police training courses in the UK for overseas police officers
Regular training courses for overseas officers have, in cooperation
with the Home Office, been organized at the following centres for
many years.

173

Appendix G

Location	Subject	Duration	Number of students per year (1977)
MP Training Centre, Hendon	General duties (twice yearly)	20 weeks	50
National Police Staff College, Bramshill House	Command and management (4 courses per year) UK command courses (3 places per year)	15 weeks	48
West Yorkshire Police Academy, Wakefield	CID operational duties (3 per year)		40
Cheshire Constabulary Training Centre, Crewe	General duties (1 course per year)		15
			153

Training was also available at the following centre in specialist subjects, in which overseas officers were integrated in existing courses for UK officers.

Location	Subject	Duration	Number of students per year (1977)
MP Training Centre, Hendon	F/P and photography	12 weeks	1
	F/print	6 weeks	2
	Photograph	12 weeks	1
Durham Police HQ	Scientific aids and scenes of crime	9 weeks	4
Staffordshire Police HQ	Crime prevention	4 weeks	4
Lancashire Police HQ	Traffic patrol duties	4 weeks	1
			13
Total			166

Index

175

Index

Index

Index

Mulligan, Jimmy, 99
Munich, 6–8, 11
Munster, Lord, 52
Muslim, 87, 142, 147
Mussolini, Benito, 1
Mutesa, Freddie, 51
Muthaiga, 22, 88
Mwarusha, 33

Nadiope, William Wilberforce, 57–8
Nagasaki, 4
Nairobi, 19, 22, 34, 47, 69–70, 77, 88, 91–2, 122, 134–5
Nakasero Hill, 89
Nakil Yaslam, 103
Nakuru, 51, 79
Namirembe Cathedral, 61
Nanking, 1–2
National Police Staff College, xv, xx, 95, 97, 174
National Union of Students, 9
Natron, Lake, 33
Nazi, 6–7, 7–10, 17–19, 118–26, 128–32
Nchanga mine, 138
Ndola, 137
Nekyon, Mr, 77
Nelson, 30
Nevis, 152–3, 155, 161–2, 173
New Africa Hotel, 134
New Mexico, 95
New York, 7, 94–5, 102
New Zealand, 29
Newara Eliya, 31
Niagara Falls, 4
Nigeria, xx, 11, 41, 54, 80, 170
Nile, 56, 67–8, 75, 78
Nile Mansions, 89
Nilotic, 41
Nimule, 67
Ningpo, 4
Njombe, 26
Nkomo, Joshua, 69
Norfolk Hotel, 69
North Katanga, 83
North-West Frontier, 109
North Yemen, 102, 104, 106; see also Yemen Arab Republic
Northern Province, 31–2, 34–5, 118, 149

Northern Rhodesia, xviii–xix, 26, 137; see also Zambia
Nsambya Barracks, 38
Nubis, 87
Nyakyusa, 26
Nyanzi, Professor Semei, 92
Nyasa, Lake, 26
Nyasaland, xviii, 35, 137–8; see also Malawi
Nyerere, Julius, 35, 72
Nyeri, 19, 33

Oberstdort, 7
Obitra-Gama, Colonel, 86
Obote, Milton, 52, 58–9, 61–2, 68, 70, 72, 76–7, 81, 86–9, 92
Obote, Miria, 61
Obwangor, 74
Office of Public Safety, 95
Ohio, 95
Okondo, Jessie, 38
Oldeani, 18
Omari, Dunstan, 36
Onama, Felix, 74–5, 84
Oraba, 65
Orientale Province, 47, 49, 54, 63–4, 82–3
Orinduik, 107–8
Orinoco, 107
Oropoi, 47
Oryema, Erinayo, 81
Ostend, 28
Ottawa, 95–6
Overseas Development Administration, xxi, 97
Owen Falls Dam, 57
Oxford University, 5–6, 8, 9, 11, 61, 94–5

Pacific, 4, 168, 171
Paghman, 113
Paignton Sands, 130
Pakistan, 109–12, 171
Palestine, xvii, 16
Pantellaria, 14
Parachute Regiment, 162
Paris, 1–2, 8, 13, 166
Paulis, 83
Pehin, 94
Penang, 1

181